Diary of Annie's War

by

Annie Dröege

**Grosvenor House
Publishing Limited**

This book is published by
Grosvenor House Publishing Ltd
28-30 High Street, Guildford, Surrey, GU1 3EL.
www.grosvenorhousepublishing.co.uk

A CIP record for this book
is available from the British Library

ISBN 978-1-908596-97-0

In memory of the 16.5 million lives lost in the Great War - including 5.7 million Allied soldiers and four million troops with the Central Powers - it is estimated that 6.8 million civilians of all countries died. The figures are frightening, but the horror of modern warfare was even more terrifying for those caught up in the conflict that ran from 1914-1918.

Wilfred Owen 1893-1918.
Dulce et Decorum est pro patria mori (it is sweet and right to die for your country – sadly the Great War's greatest poet did just that on November 4th 1918 seven days before the end of the conflict - his mother got the tragic news on Armistice Day):

My friend, you would not tell with such high zest
To children ardent for some desperate glory,
The old Lie; Dulce et Decorum est
Pro patria mori.

GREAT Aunt Annie's diary must have lain in the back of various cupboards for nearly a hundred years.

In 1940 the diary was rescued by her niece Jean Vlotman. On Aunt Jean's death the diary was given to me. In its new home it gathered more dust until it was 'rediscovered' and fondly transcribed. Together with the diary was a small photograph album containing a few aged pictures - the only other remaining record of Annie and Arthur's time in Germany.

There are many diaries from WW1 telling of the horrific times in the trenches but Annie Dröege's diary describes the lives of the civilian German people living in and around the garrison town of Hildesheim and beyond during the Great War.

Annie Dröege tells of her time as the wife of a Ruhleben internee and of being a lone Englishwoman living in the land of her country's enemy.

I have reproduced Annie's handwritten account of her time in Germany to the best of my ability. I believe with the 100th anniversary of the start of the Great War approaching that it deserves a wider audience.

The diary is a well documented reflection of the social history and lives of the families in a German garrison town during the First World War. And I believe her work is of extra interest having been penned by an Englishwoman under virtual house arrest at times.

Mark Drummond Rigg.

Annie (Drummond) Dröege

ANNIE was born in the busy market town of Stockport on July 25th, 1874. She was the eldest of her parents Anne and John Drummond's nine children. On the early death of her mother she was left with the responsibility of looking after her seven remaining brothers and sisters, aged from five to twenty, and her father.

The family was reasonably well-to-do as John worked for his mother another Annie – known as 'The Duchess of Lever Street' - at her millinery business in Manchester. Annie's grandmother exported smocks, hats, and bonnets to Germany using the local Commission Agents Dröege & Co.

Through her grandmother's business Annie first met the love of her life Arthur - the younger son of German Leopold Dröege and his English wife Elizabeth. Arthur Dröege was a British national and had been educated in England. Arthur was a leading light in the family business and befitting his position he spoke six languages fluently.

After meeting in their youth a romance blossomed and after a serious courtship Annie and Arthur wed on the 30th June 1900 at St Philip and St James' Church in Shaw Heath, Stockport, Cheshire.

In the March of 1902 their daughter Annie Josephine was born. Sadly, baby Annie Josephine died in December

1903 and then to add more heartache their son Leopold died shortly after his birth.

Arthur's father Leopold died in March 1908 and the following year Arthur's older brother Marcus died at the age of 29. This bereavement was quickly followed by another back in Germany of Arthur's uncle, a friend of Kaiser Wilhelm II, who died without issue.

Following his father's death Arthur changed careers and became a foreign correspondent working from his home in Stockport for the German press.

And after his uncle's demise, as the oldest living male relative, Arthur inherited his relative's possessions. These included a manor and vast estate in the village of Woltershausen, Lower Saxony, where the lands were let to tenant farmers. He was also heir to a house in Hildesheim, a villa by the Rhine in Königswinter and a house by the health springs in Bad Salzdetfurth.

On their arrival in Woltershausen Arthur was welcomed as the new owner and the inheritance appeared to be a fantastic opportunity. Annie was surprised and disappointed to find that the German domestic staff, though naturally polite, only regarded her as 'the Frau of Herr Dröege'.

Annie worked on her strengths and as 'the Frau of Herr Dröege' found that she could be a valuable mediator between the tenant farmers, their wives and her husband.

All was settled and uneventful until the outbreak of war in the summer of 1914.

In early November of that year Arthur was taken to Ruhleben as a German prisoner-of-war. This came about after England had refused to release prisoners of German nationality. The reason given for his imprisonment was that Arthur had an English mother. Annie, whilst expecting imprisonment, was ordered to report to the police twice daily. She was left alone to look after Arthur's affairs.

Now known as 'The Outlander' Annie was shunned by many old friends and others who knew she was English.

Many times she did have the option of returning to England but said repeatedly: 'When we leave, we leave together'.

This is her story, in her own words.

Hildesheim. November 25th – 1914

It was a suggestion of Belle van der Busch that we should take notes of these anxious days. I, especially, having plenty of time.

Though it is now sixteen weeks since the war began I think the most important events to me will easily come back to memory. So, as near as possible, I will give the dates of the events which concerned me much, for we had several very anxious days and nights.

A.D.

ANNIE'S WAR

The diary of Annie Dröege.
Germany WW1.

Sunday 26th July 1914.

Emily Durselen came to visit us - bringing with her, from England, Winnie Crocker and also Marjorie Henson. The two children were to stay six weeks and return in time for school on September 12th. James Walmsley, from Blackpool, had been with us a short time and we were a merry party for a few days.

The first we heard of the war, to take it seriously, was a letter to Emily D. from her sister, Frau Graeinghoff, of Königswinter, in which she regretted Emily and the children had come. We laughed very much at the idea because they had only been with us four days. The letter came on the Thursday morning and when the newspaper came in the afternoon Arthur thought it probable that Russia and Germany might go to war. But we were so merry we forgot all about it in a few minutes.

Friday 31st July.

Arthur, James and I went into Hildesheim. There we heard that all preparations were in hand and everyone was talking of the war. To fight Serbia and Russia meant nothing to them. So they said. If only England would keep out of it. They said they could not trust her, she was so sly.

When we got to Harbarnsen in the evening we met some of the men of our village already going away. Still James and Arthur had no fear for they were sure England would not join. They did not see how it could affect us.

Sunday 2nd August 1914.

When we were at church at Lamspringe we found the reserves had been called up, officers especially, at a few hours notice. We were left without a medical doctor and a vet surgeon. Dr. Foss was a marine officer and Dr.Kort was a field officer. It was something serious for us for they had to attend to seven or eight villages. They had to go quickly. What surprised me even then was that England was blamed for it all.

After church Arthur and James decided to go to Hildesheim and enquire if it was possible for James to leave. The trains were all being used for the transport of soldiers and we were afraid he would have difficulty in getting direct to Hamburg. They could get no definite news so Arthur telephoned from Hildesheim to the shipping office and heard that a boat would sail on Tuesday 4th August. It was decided to try for that. I posted three letters on this date to England.

Monday 3rd August.

James, Arthur and I were in Hildesheim. I shall never forget it. I saw there the crowds of young men called up to military duty. We could scarcely get any news of the trains. None of the officials knew anything. All trains being held up for transport of horses and men. At last we heard that a train was likely to go sometime after dinner and I left Arthur and James at the hotel about half past two. I went to do a little shopping and they were to go to the station.

I was very doubtful of James getting away for already the people were saying strange things about England. Arthur was doubtful also but said it was James' wish to try his luck. I called on Belle v.d. Busch and she told me that her husband's mother died on the 28th July and was buried on the 30th. Her eldest son, who is an officer, could not remain for the funeral being called away to the front the same morning.

The organisation of the German army is perfect. The vet from Lamspringe wrote that, although called up in a few hours notice, every man's outfit and every horse's harness was quite complete. Each man was fitted up in a few minutes and every buckle in its place on the harness. The shoemaker from our village said he was at once put to his trade in the barracks. They turned out three thousand pairs of shoes a day. The butcher also was called and he was kept busy at his trade. The supply of men was wonderful. Each train that came in was crowded with men. There was a man on each platform who directed them to their respective barracks and one saw no confusion at all.

After the regular army had gone away (many thousands) there came the 'free willing' which consisted of men over thirty years old and men under twenty years old. Those under twenty had to drill and these over thirty only needed a couple of weeks and then they were ready. So many came that they could not accept them all and many thousands were told to present themselves again in a month.

When we returned home on the Monday evening after seeing James on his journey to Hamburg we found a notice saying that Arthur must take the horse, 'Moor', to Alfeld on the Thursday August 6th. We had already had warning that he must be in readiness the Saturday before.

Tuesday 4th August.

The day found us very anxiously awaiting the reply from England. At noon we got a card from James saying that he got to Hamburg all right and hoped to sail on Tuesday. He told us that the ship that sailed on the Saturday had been turned back. When Arthur heard that he said James would not sail until England had answered Germany. If the answer was unfavourable the ship would not sail at all. We were very miserable that night for the uncertainty was dreadful and the people were saying awful things about England.

Wednesday 5th August.

We drove to Lamspringe, Arthur and I alone, for there was a special Mass at six o'clock in the morning for the soldiers at the front. As we drove through the villages of Graste and Netze I remarked to Arthur the unwillingness of the men to open the barriers which were across the roads at the entrance to every village. These barriers had been put up the first day of the war and at each was a man, sometimes two men, with a loaded gun. Their duty was to examine every strange cart or person who came along. If they knew you they often had the barrier open as you got to them. This morning however they made us pull up the horse and then slowly undid the barrier.

Going into Lamspringe there was quite a lot of men and they let us wait a few seconds before they let us pass.

Arthur thanked them but they made no reply. I felt nervous for we had to go the same way back. When I looked at Arthur I was surprised to see how pale he had gone. I think we both feared war with England had been declared. But we never mentioned it to each other.

We left the carriage at the hotel and went into Mass. It upset me very much. Nearly everyone was crying, for so many men had been called up. Wives were crying because their husbands had gone. And the little ones were crying because they saw their mothers cry. I often thought of that morning when I was in church afterwards. So many men who were going away went to communion.

It was a perfect August day.

When we got to the hotel after Mass Arthur went to give his instructions over his horse 'Moor' and I heard 'The Bellman' in the road. After his announcement the people hissed at me and I felt afraid. Just at that moment the wife of the innkeeper came out and said we had better wait a while as there were many horses coming along with recruits from Bad Gandersheim. They were on their way to Hannover for the war and it was better to let them get past for they also had wagons.

It was very sad to see them. There were one hundred and seventy-eight wagons. Each wagon with two horses in the front and many with two horses fastened behind. They were driven by recruits from the same town and a couple of soldiers on horseback rode up and down by their sides to direct. Several of the drivers were young teachers and you could see that they had never driven before. The others were young farmers. The people were upset at seeing this procession for it meant that the farmers were without horses, wagons and men and it was harvest month. It was to be a very good harvest this year. They knew when the larger towns and villages had been called upon, and then it was their turn. No wonder they felt very angry with us. For some unexplained reason England was blamed for Russia and France going to war. France, they told us, never declared war but at England's advice commenced to drop bombs on Germany.

As we drove home we met the same angry crowd at the barriers but not a word was spoken. Afterwards we heard that it was the intention of some of them to stone us as we passed. In fact the report was spread that it had actually happened.

When we got to the house Emily met us with alarming news. She had packed her boxes and wanted to be off. Mrs. Steinoff had been talking to her in the garden and had told her how very angry people had become on hearing war had been declared with England. We were the only foreigners in that district and of course we were the object of all their spite. They said that if England joined France and Russia they were done. All their threats were for England. Mrs. Steinoff said the people were more angry with me than Herr Dröege. It was because he said he would like to live there all winter, and I had said I never would do so. So it showed all my thoughts were for England etc. etc.

Emily had been in the kitchen and the cook had told her that she had heard so much of what the people had said in the village. George the coachman had been there and told her what they said. She was afraid of staying at nights and was sure they meant to attack us or set fire to the place. She also said that early that morning she had been getting some apples in the garden near the road and two men passing had made the remark, 'This house looks fine now, but I don't think tomorrow will see it so fine looking'.

She refused to stay all night and went home to sleep. We decided it was perhaps better that the children and Emily went away. So we continued with the packing. But on enquiries after dinner we found it impossible to send them away as all the trains were stopped. In fact we were two weeks and had no trains at all.

After a long talk together Arthur decided to go and see the man who occupies the position of 'mayor' to the village. I went into the kitchen with Emily to write some letters. The children were a little afraid for they had heard of the 'chat' in the village.

Louise, the cook, was very upset when I got into the kitchen and at once implored me to get away. She said she was sure harm was intended for us and if we only knew the talk in the village we should go at once. I did not take much notice of her because she was very much upset on her own account over the war. Her lover and her brother had been called up three days before and I thought a great deal of her crying was because she was in so much trouble. I told her I was not afraid and that I had a very much higher opinion of the German people than she evidently had. I reminded her we had never had any unpleasantness from the villagers. She replied that the war made the men mad for they all knew they must go and fight. She ended by remarking that she did not consider it safe for herself and should not sleep in the house at night. But Johanna Matties, the other servant, said she was not afraid. There the matter ended for the kitchen.

I went into the garden, meeting on my way the postman with a letter from James Walmsley saying he was still in Hamburg and that he had been on the ship since Monday . It was now Tuesday evening and they were afraid they would not get away.

As I was reading it Mrs. Steinoff came out and told me a lot of the news she had given Emily. I said I was surprised at it and did not expect it of our people. She said all people are bad in war times and she felt a little afraid. On Steinoff coming along and hearing our talk I noticed she did not express herself as afraid. Steinoff himself laughed at us but said the people were very angry at England who had caused Russia and France to go to war with them (the Germans).

Half an hour later Arthur came in and I could see he was upset. I went into his room and he told me of a very remarkable thing. He said he was sitting talking to Herr Scharfer (the mayor) when a man came in and Arthur got up to leave the room. The man said: 'What I have to say you can hear. I will say it to your face'.

Then he made a statement demanding that our house was searched from top to bottom. He believed we were spies and had bombs concealed. He also said he had heard that Arthur had remarked: 'If we had any annoyance he would throw a bomb in the village'.

This remark was supposed to have been made when Arthur had found an apple tree stripped of its fruit. Arthur immediately asked the mayor to come to our place and search. He remarked that the doors had been open to all since early morning and that, as far as we knew, there had been no apple tree robbed of its fruit, nor had there been. It was a tale ready made up. Of course the mayor refused to do what was asked.

Arthur came home and we talked the matter over. I suggested we telephoned for the police officer at

Lamspringe to come at once and hear the details of the case. I felt afraid when I knew we were taken for spies. Among such people, and in war time, it was not a very nice position. Also we must remember that the nearest police station was four-and-a-half miles away and the house stands alone.

The principal thing was that these people who had made the accusation were workers at the Kali mines and were in a position to get explosives. I told Arthur there was nothing to prevent them getting what they wanted and then putting the articles in our house. It would be serious if they were found.

Arthur telephoned the police and a very smart officer was with us in half an hour. He was so very thoughtful and kind. He remarked that it was his duty to protect us and we could rely on him doing his best, but he had a deal to do. He had heard we had many Socialists in our village and at once put it down to them - which proved true.

He got at the man who had spoken to Arthur and it appeared the same man had been called up that morning to his military and that had not pleased him. The officer went into various pubs in the village and said if we had any annoyance he would make the parties pay for it. I do not think it made any impression. At six o'clock Louise the cook went home to sleep, but Johanna decided to sleep in her own room. We were not a very happy household that night.

Thursday 6th August.

We were up very early for Arthur had to take 'Moor' to Alfeld and he was to take George with him. I might say I was not pleased at the prospect of being alone in the place without a man. We had heard the previous evening that the people had said they would stone us the first time they met us in the streets.

I also remembered that the people knew that Arthur was going to Alfeld, for several others from the village had to go also. I did not feel any better when Arthur came into the room and remarked: 'They have cut the telephone in the night and we cannot telephone'.

That showed, I thought, that they were not going to be afraid of the police. We scarcely knew what to do. Arthur and George had to go away early. Emily, I and the children would have felt a little more secure knowing we could telephone to the police. However, Steinoff came in from the fields before Arthur went away and he went up to the public house in the village. He telephoned from there to the general post of in Lamspringe and told them of what had happened.

It proved to be a great blessing in disguise. In about half an hour an official from the post office came and he raved and stormed all over the place. I heard that in the village he had quite frightened the people by telling them what lay in wait for the people who had done it. After him came the police officer. He went to the mayor and written notices were issued asking the people to give all information. The telephone was not 'Herr Dröege's' but it was 'The Kaiser's' and the man who had cut it was an enemy of the government. The telephone official had remarked in the village that the man who had done it would be shot at once. No one told us who it was. The police officer remarked that now that had happened he would have to come each night and walk for so long round the house.

Arthur came home about half past five and all was in order. He had had a talk with the magistrate in Alfeld and he said he should send a notice to six villages around Woltershausen warning the people not to molest us as we were peaceful. We were told that the telephone would be on night and day for us and we felt a little more secure. George also went into the village in the evening and said the talk had stopped.

Friday 7th August.

Many of the men went away. Among them the man Rutt who had charged us with having bombs.

We got a postcard from James Walmsley saying they had not got away. In fact the boat that had set out on the Saturday before war was declared on the Tuesday had been turned back and they were still in Hamburg.

The succeeding days brought us no peace as everything in the papers was against the English, and the talk was awful. We had to keep the children in the garden and did not often go out ourselves. George offered himself for the war, he had the age to go in October, and there was not much work for him with the horse gone.

We were very glad of news. We only saw one paper and it did not give us consolation.

On the following Sunday we walked to church and found that Pastor Gatsemire had returned. He was on holiday when the war broke out. He was in Spain when the news reached him. A ship at once set out for Hamburg and he said if they had been four hours later it would have been too late to get away. They passed a ship that had struck a mine that same morning - the first sea loss we read of. They had to have a special pilot who knew were the mines were laid. He had a very exciting twenty-four hours on the sea and we were very glad to have him back.

After a week or so we got a train, put on early in the morning, but the service was dreadful. The telephone and telegraph also were held up so many hours a day. Each day we got a postcard from James telling us of how he was fixed. We mentioned his case to the police official but he said not to send for him to stay at Woltershausen. Arthur telephoned to Hildesheim and told the head waiter at Weiner Hof that he had advised James to come there. The head waiter replied that it was not safe as they had a deal of trouble with two Americans who were there. The people were suspicious and the police had been to see them. He strongly advised James to stay in a large town. Arthur wrote to that effect.

It was a difficult matter writing to James for we did not want to tell him too much of our unpleasantness. At last he wrote us he had got decent lodgings and he was staying in Hamburg. At this time James' postcards were all we lived on for we had no other news. Each day brought us anxiety and so we went on for a couple of weeks.

Monday 10th August.

James' postcards to his father and to Fr. Blundell were returned. He had sent them on Sunday the 2nd. I received also a letter back sent to Mrs. Hopkins also posted on the 2nd. The one written to father and one to Mrs. Ralphs never returned. I often wonder if they got them.

We were very glad during those days that we had the children and Emily though we spent all our time in the garden having no trains to go anywhere and the horse gone away. We had to walk to Mass each Sunday for we could not borrow an animal. All had gone to the war with the exception of very old working horses.

Thursday 20th August.

We got a letter from Herr Steffen in Limburg to say there was no business doing and that if he could get a train he should come to stay with us and so fulfil a long promised visit. It was almost two weeks before he could travel. We had several letters and telegrams announcing his arrival and then - 'No Trains Tomorrow'.

Wednesday 26th August.

Arthur went to Hildesheim for a train went through our station in the morning. He scarcely knew when he would return but he said: 'Surely before dark'. We went down the road at eight o'clock and waited almost an hour. Then we returned home. Emily and I were very nervous but still hoped that nothing had happened. Arthur came home a little after twelve o'clock and he had to cycle from Hildesheim. I resolved to go with him next time. The journey was better than the anxiety at home.

Tuesday 1st September 1914.

The cook left us. Emily and I were kept busy in the kitchen for some weeks after this. George the coachman had gone into the army on the 26th of August so we were a little less in the house. Johanna was a great help and we could get a woman from the village when necessary. We managed very well. I think Emily and I were pleased to have something to do. We had less time to worry.

Sunday 5th September.

Herr Steffen came, and we were glad to see him. He said he had come for a long stay as the war had stopped their trade. I was glad for Arthur's sake.

We had a card from James and he had a plan for getting away. We had heard that the route through Holland was opened so we wished him luck. The next morning there came a paper cutting from Mrs. Durselen saying that a number of English people had been arrested on the borders of Holland. They were trying to get away and had been imprisoned. We were very anxious over James for a few days. But at last came a card from Holland and we felt surer of him then getting home.

Things were getting quieter in our village but we heard rumours of a deal of talk against the English in the other villages. Each night we took more care of the doors. Emily and the children slept on the third floor and constantly said that they saw lights and heard people in the garden.

Herr Steffen also said that he heard people at his end of the house once or twice, but we never did. Several times Emily came downstairs and said there were people in the shrubbery, but we never saw them. However on the night of the 9th of September, the Wednesday after Herr Steffen came, I was fast asleep also Arthur. I heard a knock at our room door. I heard Emily saying: 'Get up at once. There are people smashing windows and bursting in doors'.

Arthur was up in a minute and we went to the door of Herr Steffen's room. He was asleep. Though we could hear the glass crashing and the banging of the door, he never heard it. He at once jumped up and we all made our way into Arthur's room. The people were in front of the house and we could hear their voices. Herr Steffen asked Arthur if his gun was loaded. Arthur said, 'only his revolver'.

We were in the dark for we did not want the people to locate the room we were in. In fact, I do not think they had any idea we were up. Now, from the time of the telephone affair, we had been given permission to shoot any one who came on our premises to annoy us.

In fact it was given out at church that if Herr Droege had been annoyed then he must shoot anyone who came in his grounds for an unlawful purpose. It was just a month that night since the telephone was cut. Herr Steffen made no bother over shooting anyone. He just took up the revolver and saw that the six chambers were full. He then opened the window and asked: 'What are you doing there?'

The reply came: 'Come out and we will kill you'.

'Oh yes', said Herr Steffen and fired at once. They could not see exactly were he was for there are fifteen windows on that side of the house and we had no lights on in the place. He fired five times and then Arthur told him to keep one bullet in readiness. We waited, but no more noises were heard.

Arthur opened a window in his room and we could see Steinoffs were up. So I called to them. They were afraid at first for they thought that the shots came from the garden but they felt safer when they knew they were from the house. We then had a good look around but could not see anyone. Emily, I and the children were in Arthur's room and the men went round the gardens and grounds. About a quarter of an hour later Steinoff's servant said she could hear men talking on the Harlainsen road. We came to the conclusion that they had gone there.

We telephoned the police and a reply came that the officer would come up in a short time. It was just a quarter to two when Emily awoke us and the officer got there at three. We were very disappointed to find it was a stranger. The officer we had over the telephone affair was a far smarter man.

The new officer heard our tale and said that he would cycle around and come again early in the daylight. He had the impression that it had been a few men out of the village. It was the reason that the dogs did not bark. That was a strange affair. I cannot yet understand it. Arthur had bought an English Retriever, a very well bred animal, and he was asleep in Arthur's room. In the farmyard was Dolar, a very good watchdog of Steinoff's, and by our door was Valder in his kennel. Not one of our animals had barked. It was only when the noise was over that we thought of them. They had to be brought out of their kennels. Lord, in the house, quietly walked about but never seemed to really waken up. It was a thing that surprised us all.

When we were quiet enough for a talk it seemed that both Emily and Marjorie had seen the men come in the garden. Emily said she had been awakened by a loud crash. She got up and went to the window to look out. She saw two or three men by the private gate and when they found it locked they went to the gate leading into the farmyard. This they placed open and then went to the little garden gate leading to our house from the farmyard. We had put a spring on this door so it would close. They then carefully unhooked the spring.

One went to the door and commenced to bang on it and the two others commenced to throw stones at the windows.

We gathered over sixty stones the next morning and a few had gone through the window into the room where they first attacked. They had not cared to face the revolver and had soon cleared off. It was strange, but I had never really felt afraid. I think it is only when you are not sure of danger that you get nervous. I had felt much more nervous on the Wednesday when war was declared than I did when the men were smashing the windows. I knew this night what we had to face. I felt there was danger unknown.

As soon as the firing and stone throwing ceased I laughed to myself. It was the picture we made. Emily, the children and I were all standing in Arthur's room in our nightgowns and bare feet. Johanna ditto but she had put a dress on. Arthur and Herr Steffen had been in nightshirts and socks when running about with a gun and a revolver. It was a little funny to me. But no one else saw that side of the picture. I do not mean the occasion was a thing to laugh at. It was the figures we cut that made me laugh.

The children were terrified and it was a long time before they forgot it. One day they presented us with a piece of poetry they had written about the night. I am sorry it was put on the fire.

The police never found the men but I do not think it is any one out of our village. We heard afterwards that the same thing happened the first week of the war to a couple living in Bad Salzdetfurth. The shock had killed the wife of the man. They were French people but he had been naturalised a German and had been in the employ of the railway for over seventeen years. All their windows were broken in the night but the police never found the persons. And that house stood on a street. We came to the conclusion that the people came either from Sehlem or Salzdetfurth, two villages four and six miles away, but it is only our opinion. We never went to bed without the men having loaded guns.

After this we were very quiet and very busy for the fruit was ripe. We could not hire help to get it in.

Herr Steffen's niece came the Monday following and stayed two weeks so we were very merry once more. The three young people in the house kept us alive.

The three children did a deal of work in the garden gathering (and eating) fruit. For three or four weeks Arthur and 'Uncle George', as we all called Herr Steffen, were very busy. Once in this time Arthur and Emily and again, Arthur and Herr Steffen and I, went into Hildesheim but it took us four and a half hours to get home. We were not anxious to go often. Theresa Steffen was with us for two weeks and then she returned to her grandmother in Hildesheim to await Herr Steffen going home.

About the middle of September we found there would be no going home this side of Christmas. It was decided to send the children to school. Many had remarked over their not going to school in the village and a child is not allowed to reside in a place more than six weeks without schooling. We wrote to Mrs. Graeinghoff and asked her to find a school for the children. Arthur and I thought of a boarding school but it was not possible. After a lot of trouble on the part of Mrs. Graeinghoff it was decided to send them to a private school and let Emily stay with them in a pension. It was very good of Emily to offer to do so. She could have gone to stay with her cousins in Elberfeldt – but she thought of the children.

Wednesday 23rd September.

We heard of the three English boats being sunk, the **Aboukir, Hogue** and **Cressy.** It was reported here that though it only happened at seven o'clock most of the men saved had only their night clothes on, and were asleep at the time. We said it was strange for men to be asleep at seven o'clock during war time.

Sunday 27th September.

We heard that a German flyer had thrown a bomb at the Eiffel Tower. We also heard of all the German victories in Belgium.

We got a letter from Johanna Pulmann (a cousin of Arthur) asking us if we had any news of England. She was very upset over her married daughter in London. She also wrote us that cousin Franceska, who we had visited in Brussels last November, has had to flee from her home. They had received no news of Franceska or her daughter-in-law for two weeks and then heard they had arrived in Holland.

Both their homes had been destroyed. Cousin Franceska's three sons were in the war for Germany and had been called up a week before the entry of Brussels. I suppose this fact had annoyed the Belgians. We were very thankful to find they were safe for we had often thought of them.

During the month of October we lived very quietly at Woltershausen. 'Uncle George' and Arthur were very busy with the garden and fruit. I had enough to do with the cook being away.

We heard of many German victories also of the English ship '**The Hawk**' sinking a German boat.

Tuesday 29th September.

Arthur and I went with the children to Hildesheim on a very early train, a quarter to six, and we had coffee in Hildesheim. We walked round and did some shopping for the children and paid a visit to Frau v.d. Busch. After dinner we saw the children and Emily on a train for Elberfeldt where they were to stay the night and then they were to go on to Königswinter. We saw a lot of soldiers going off to France and many fine horses. The men were very lively and sang their songs all the time they were in the station. We caught a train half an hour after them but it took us almost four hours to get home.

While Emily was with us she had written to a friend in Holland and had sent a letter to her sister. We were able to hear that all our people were well. Also that James was safe at home. We received in September a notice from the American Consul asking of the children and James. We replied that the children were safe and that James had returned home.

Wednesday 28th October 1914.

Uncle George left and we were sorry to part with him. It was quite a business getting him away for he took so much 'livestock' with him - a dog, chickens, a duck and a canary.

The place was very quiet after he had gone. But we were busy with our packing and making ready to go ourselves. We had arranged to go to Hildesheim for a week or so, finish our business from there, and then go to Königswinter for the Christmas.

We had been under police surveillance since the telephone was cut and all our letters came and went through them. Of course they must be opened.

Arthur had business to attend to in Hildesheim on the 30th of October so we decided to come in the town on that date. We settled up with Johanna. She had another situation to go to on the 1st of November and left Woltershausen on the evening of the 29th.

Things were much better in Hildesheim though there was, and is still, a very bitter feeling against England. Many of the shops have notices saying not to ask for any English produce. We had hardly got there when we were put under notice of the police.

We heard that the German prisoners were being very badly treated in England and some dreadful tales were told in the newspapers. Then we heard that Germany had sent word to England that if she did not release the Germans who were imprisoned then Germany would do the same with her English people. We awaited anxiously for the reply. We were very much surprised to read in the papers that England had only laughed at the message and said it was a German bluff and never answered at all.

Friday 6th November 1914.

By noon all the English people were arrested and imprisoned.

I had been very uneasy all week but Arthur had laughed at me and remarked that we had no need to fear.

I reminded him of the fix I should be in if he were taken. I insisted on him going to the bank and getting a certain sum of money. He was not in any hurry to do so as he did not think for one moment that the Englishmen would be arrested. He also remarked that even if they did arrest the Englishmen then they would give the people a few hours notice to get ready. I asked him how he knew that. I drew his attention to the fact that this war was different to any other. Therefore he must not rely on what had happened at other times.

I was in a shop that morning and saw the police arrest a workman there. Belle was with me and we made enquiries. I learned he was an Englishman but had lived the best part of his life in Germany. In fact he could not speak English for he came here when he was only two-years-old. I felt very much alarmed and hurried back to the hotel. There they told me Arthur had not yet come in. I knew he had gone to meet a decorator at the house in Wörth Strasse so I awaited him. He came in about one o'clock and I at once said what I had seen. He said he did not think it would come to him but afterwards told me that a gentleman from the bank had spoken to him in the street. Arthur had replied that he must take his chance.

At a quarter past one we went into the dining room and I noticed how very quickly the dinner was served. They scarcely waited until we had finished the soup when the next course was on the table. Just as we finished the meal the waiter came and told Arthur he was wanted in the hall. I thought at once that it was the police.

Arthur came back in a few minutes and said that he must go away. I was not so much surprised. We went upstairs and hurriedly packed a few things. Herr Roeder, the proprietor, was very kind and told us what to pack and what to leave out. He said it was no use packing nightclothes but Arthur must have a couple of rugs and a pillow. These he found for us. In a quarter-of-an-hour Arthur was away. I just felt as if I was walking in a dream. I could not realise he was gone and I alone in a hotel. However, about three o'clock I went round to see Belle and after a chat I felt much more reconciled.

I felt very indignant with England for not even having the manners to reply to Germany.

Saturday 7th November.

I heard that Arthur was in Hannover having gone there in an auto on the Friday night. He had asked permission of the police to go alone with an officer and it was granted. Belle and I went to the station about five o'clock thinking that the prisoners might go on the train about that time. We did not see anything of them. And we did not care to ask.

One has to be very careful these days not to draw attention to the fact that you are a foreigner. We were afraid to speak English in the streets. When I returned to the hotel about seven o'clock there was a note from the police saying that I must go to the office and announce myself twice a day. My times were ten – twelve in the morning, and from three – four in the afternoon. This was changed after to four – six in the evening. Sundays and holidays it was eleven – twelve mornings, and three – four afternoons. Several times I was on the last minute, for I used to forget.

Monday 9th November.

I wrote to Emily saying I was alone. She replied that they had heard from Otto Klein and they were afraid he also was imprisoned.

I had a postcard from Arthur in which he said they were all together from various parts of the province. He thought they would go to Berlin on the Sunday. We read afterwards in the papers of an account of the send off of the prisoners from Hannover on the Sunday afternoon.

My next postcard came from Ruhleben and Arthur asked for several things to be sent to him. He had sent the postcard to me at Belle's address and I answered at once that I would send them off. I had to take my postcard to the police and they had to read it before posting.

In about two hours after me leaving it with them I received a notice to go to the police again. They had read in the postcard of me having had one from Arthur. Since it had not gone to my address, 'The Weiner Hof', they had not read it. I explained that my husband had sent it to the address of a cousin as he thought it should have gone there. They told me to write at once and tell him that I was still at the hotel. If I received any letters unknown to the police then I would be put in prison. We wrote at once to Arthur and told him to be particular to where he addressed his cards. He is only allowed to write postcards – me also.

I take all my correspondence to the police and they read it and then they post it opened. I must go twice a day to report myself morning and afternoon. I must be in my dwelling no later than eight o'clock in the evening and I must not leave before seven o'clock in the morning.

I must not go more than two-and-a-quarter miles away from home. There are eleven in all who must report themselves daily in Hildesheim.

I believe that there were seven men arrested. Most were Germans naturalised in England or the sons of men who were naturalised. The question was: 'Have you served in the army?'

None of the naturalised men had done so.

Hildesheim is a garrison town and the number of soldiers one meets on the streets is really remarkable. Up to the middle of November nearly twenty-five thousand soldiers have been sent out of Hildesheim and the streets are always full.

I saw a lot of soldiers ready for the front one day. You can tell when they are going away. On their last day their helmets are covered and the numbers taken off their arms and sewn inside their jackets. Every soldier I met seemed ready to go and I thought the town would be empty of men in the morning. I had been told two thousand and seven hundred were to go away that day. The next day the place was full of blue uniforms and you never missed the men in grey.

The soldiers are splendidly fitted up and want for nothing. When the cold weather set in they were provided with corduroy trousers and woollen under jackets. Just like the old knitted cardigans so much worn in England a few years ago. The complete outfit is a dark grey – even to scarf and gloves. The shoes are dark tan and have Wellington tops nearly to the knee. A regiment of men going away is a fine sight. There is not a speck of colour to be seen. In the distance they look just like a grey cloud. I heard that even the spurs were blacked because when the sun shone they glittered.

Often I have seen a few hundred young men come in for inspection. There are placards at the stations telling them where to go. They are then examined and towards noon you see crowds of them going into a large building where they get their clothes.

These are the clothes left behind by the soldiers who got their grey uniforms the day they left for the front. These old blue uniforms had to be well cleaned and given up on the day the men received the grey ones. They are quite ready. The men are then billeted out on various householders. According to the size of your house you have so many.

Our house in Wörth Strasse must have three soldiers. They must be up and have a cup of coffee and be at the barracks by six o'clock. They return to dinner at noon and go away at one o'clock. They get home at various times. If they are only drilling they are home at six o'clock for supper.

If they are on a march the time varies. Often they are put on a night march. They set off about eight or nine in the evening and march ten or twelve miles. They make a meal just as if they are in the battlefield and then return early in the morning. I often hear them pass the hotel and sometimes it pours with rain all the time.

After a month here they are sent away, perhaps to Goslar, to finish for two or three weeks then they are ready for the front. George (the coachman) was at the front in seven weeks after leaving us.

It makes me sad to see the young men come in. They are all sorts. Tradesmen, clerks, farmers, shop assistants etc. and you can tell them in a minute. Then there is the boy from the comfortable home who is well fitted out and looking quite contented. I often wonder how many of them have left aching hearts at home. Many sad tales are told of old parents left without one son at home. One family has five sons at the front.

Hildesheim is a beautiful town but in these dreadful days and a very sad place to live in. The beer garden was turned into a nursing camp in a very short time and every big concert hall has been fitted up with beds. They send the cases here that are not too severe and the men that can stand a train journey.

I often wonder if the women of England are working as the German women work for her soldiers. Every woman is knitting something and every child ditto. The amount of stockings, cuffs, scarves, jackets, stomach binders, knee warmers and ear covers that are knitted in a week here in Hildesheim is simply enormous. Every shop is full of grey wool and everywhere you go the people are doing something for the soldiers.

I went into a shop the other day and every young lady assistant was knitting. On the railway train it is the same; always grey wool. The shops are doing nothing in the way of business, only in such things as is necessary for the soldiers. You can get anything in the food line ready made up for the field.

A young lady told me they had given her brother enough food for a fortnight and it was all packed in a fifty cigar box - tea, sugar and rum (ready for hot water) and all kinds of soup and coffee. Cocoa is in small 'wurfels', the size of a lump of sugar, and all of the best. Small quantities of butter, sausage, meats, tongue and fish, enough for one meal, are all nicely packed up. It really is a treat to see how the soldiers are catered for.

Food up to the end of November is no dearer though there have been notices that flour (white) is getting short.

The government has issued notices forbidding a rise in the price of eatables.

Two shopkeepers, here in Hildesheim, put up the price of sugar and coffee in the second week of the war. The police got to know of it and they were at once ordered to close up their shops. Later a few shopkeepers refused to accept paper money and a notice was issued that such people were liable for imprisonment.

Within the second week of the war there was no gold to be seen. All was paper money. For the first few weeks all corn etc. was held up by the government and the farmers were not allowed to sell any until the soldiers were well provided for. Then they could dispose of what was left. But only at the same price the government gave. It was very fair for it allowed everyone to get a little. It was the same when the paraffin oil gave out. There was no rise in the price but the shopkeepers were not allowed to sell to any one person more than a pint. So everyone got a little. It was not a question of one offering double money and getting the most.

There was a very good harvest of corn and potatoes, and fruit was very plentiful. Also the government was very kind to the farmers. Before taking the horses away from the farms they asked how much land you farmed and left you a horse or two according to the size of the place. When a farmer was called up, as in the case of the Steinoff's' son-in-law, he told them he had so much land and no one to take charge. He was allowed to go back for one month and get in the harvest. On presenting himself again he was told he would be sent for when necessary. Up to the end of November the farmer was not called up. It rather surprised me for he is a fine fellow. He is in the reserves and about thirty-seven years of age. The men they were most keen about were those who left the army about five or six years ago. They required scarcely any training and were ready for the front in a week or two.

Wednesday 11th November.

I received a postcard from Arthur from Ruhleben. He said that there were all sorts and conditions of men put together. He said that it was far from agreeable. He complained of the cold and I sent him at once some thick underclothes.

Thursday 12th November.

I got a postcard from Emily, and later a telegram, in which she said she was coming to have a talk with me. She arrived on Saturday the14th, eight days after Arthur had gone, but did not get here till nine-thirty at night for there are not any through trains to Köln.

I was glad to have her if only for the nights. I had not slept three hours each night since Arthur had left. I often thought of the nights at Woltershausen when I had to go to bed at nine-thirty for I could not keep awake. It used to be a great joke amongst us. I would have given a lot for one of those nights. In my room every night from eight o'clock in the evening I heard every hour strike till six o'clock in the morning. Then when the first tram car came down I would sleep until nine or so. Emily's company was very acceptable to me and she stayed six days.

She had an idea that we could get Arthur free if she went to see the General Commander. After a talk with Herr Forster, our lawyer, she went to Hannover and there saw the General Commander. I had no faith in the affair from the first. I do not think it did any good. But we had the satisfaction of knowing we had done our best.

Monday 16th November.

Emily went to Woltershausen and said what she thought of the people there. She told the Steinoffs that the people in the Rhine district were astonished and that they scarcely believed her. She said a lot I think.

Wednesday 18th November.

The Herr Pastor of Woltershausen called to see me. I noticed one thing. Not one person, with the exception of the Steinoffs and Herminie Steffen, said they were very sorry for either Arthur or I. All made the same remark: 'So Herr Droege is in Ruhleben. You must thank your abominable government for that. He will be better treated than England treats our men'.

I said to one man: 'I would far rather he was in England as a German prisoner'.

Also many ladies told me I should be thankful I was in Germany during the war as in England they were starving. They also told me that the Germans were constantly dropping bombs in the towns on the coast.

Once or twice I said a little. As on the occasion when one person said they had a letter from a German soldier, captive in England, and his description of the place was awful - seventeen deaths in a fortnight through overcrowding. I said I didn't believe that at all. In the first place the letter would not have been allowed out of England. But I soon learned to hold my tongue.

A member of my family once said I had a great amount of adaptability. But it needed more than I had in stock to meet the present requirements.

During Emily's visit a long list of things came from Arthur which must go off at once as the prisoners were not allowed to get a parcel after the 20th. The last day of postage was the 18th. We had only one day to do it in and much to buy. It was a blessing I had Emily. In all we sent out six parcels with all he asked for and more besides.

Arthur wrote that he had met Otto Klein and they were working on the parcels that came through the post. Each had to be searched and then they made them up again. He wrote for heavy shoes so I got a pair. I also sent his forest shoes from the house. Emily had brought a lot of things with her when she went to Woltershausen.

There must have been a lot of delay over the post from Ruhleben for the postcard from Arthur was posted on the 9th and I did not get it till the 18th. It made a deal to do in a short time. We sent two parcels by express and they cost two-40 marks. A telegram that Emily sent to Arthur on the Monday 16th November had a reply post paid but we never got an answer.

Emily went back to Königswinter on Friday the 20th. The children were at Mrs. Graeinghoffs during her visit here.

Friday 20th November 1914.

Over two thousand soldiers had left Hildesheim for Russia at twenty-four hours notice. I was in the hotel corridor at eight o'clock in the morning of the 20th and heard a soldier talking to an officer who was in his bedroom. The officer was very astonished at being called to the barracks so early for he had been out on a night march. But the order was for the front and before night the whole company who had made the night march were on their way to Russia.

In the next few days we heard that the Russians had been again in Germany. But they had been beaten back. In one day the Germans had over sixty thousand prisoners and forty-two big guns taken. The next few days also brought many Russian victories. The weather at this time was very cold, five degrees of frost, so the men were very well prepared.

Two motor cars went from this hotel on the morning of the 23rd to the Russian field. They were a sight to see. Everywhere was fur. Shoes, cap, cover, jacket, gloves all were fur and the motors were the latest in comfort. They were for service. But they also took packets of cigars etc. to the soldiers from their friends.

Saturday 21st November.

Belle got a letter from the police so she went to see them. But on saying that her husband had done his military service they decided that she was a German. You take your husband's nationality here. We were thankful to hear it.

At this time it was reported that the women were to be imprisoned. I went to the bank one day and saw the manager. He told me to prepare as he was afraid it would come to me. I was not at all upset. I began to think that it would not be so lonely with someone to speak English to. Then we heard that two neutral gentlemen were to go to England and see how the people were treated there and to see if the women and children were imprisoned in England. There were some awful stories told of the cruelty of the English and the things said in the papers were dreadful.

Everything was the English. They spoke of the poor Russian, the gallant Frenchman, but it was the beast of the Englishman. One day a man turned to me, after reading something in the paper to the detriment of the English and said: 'Your husband is an Englander is he not?'

I said: 'He is just the same as your Kaiser - a German father and an English mother'.

He walked off. In such times I wonder where my adaptability has gone to. Some of the people were kind and others not. The bitterness was terrible.

In the schools the children asked not to have English lessons. The people who could speak English remarked they would try to forget it and would never speak it again. These were the better classes and middle aged people. You can imagine the outspoken feelings of the commoner classes. The Kaiser himself, in addressing the troops, said only the Bayerns were fit to meet the English in war as they were so cruel. In them the English would meet their masters.

There was a great talk of the dum-dum bullet being used by the English (these were soft point bullets that expanded on impact causing bigger wounds. In 1898 the German government had successfully campaigned for them to be banned for violating the laws of war). In fact it said in the paper that English soldiers had been taken prisoners with the bullets on them. If it is true then England deserves to lose. For that is not warfare.

Sunday 22nd November.

There was a great deal of talk about the women being taken prisoners. I thought I had better make enquiries. I asked first at the police and they said it all depended on England. If they found, after the visit of the two neutral men, that women were imprisoned in England then we should be also in Germany. I went down to the bank on this information and asked Herr Mejerhof what he thought of it. His advice was to get everything ready as he thought it very likely that the German women in England had been ordered to leave the principal towns and ports. I got several things together and bought some thick clothing.

However there was a very good report from England and for a time we are at rest.

Thursday 26th November.

We had a telephone message from Steinoff. All well at the Gut but he reported that George Machareensuar, the coachman, had been killed in France. I was sorry for we were fond of him. He had been three years at Woltershausen with us. So many young men fell about this time. Kort v.d. Busch was killed on the 28th of October and was buried on the 9th November in Hannover. His father was fighting in the same district and was able to put his son's body in a coffin and send it to his mother for burial. He was eighteen years of age.

Tuesday 1st December.

There is a notice in the paper to be very careful with flour and not to buy sweet cakes and fine bread. We are to buy brown bread and then the flour will last longer.

I wrote to Arthur today and Belle copied it in German for I have been told I was not allowed English.

I often wish for a line from England as we get no news whatsoever. Emily said, when here, that she had a letter from her sister Lena and things were very bad in England. I can think they are for in business centres here all is at a standstill. In Arthur's last postcard he wrote me he has written to Herr M. Mourrough in Lincoln, and also to my brother-in-law Bob Whittaker. He had asked the latter to send him his birth certificate and our marriage lines. I hope the postcards arrive safely.

I sent a postcard to my brother on the 2nd of November but I doubt if it got to Holland. The post officials are getting much stricter.

Friday 4th December.

We hear that Belgrade has fallen. With what losses we have not yet heard.

I sent a postcard to Arthur and a letter to Emily. Belle also wrote to Arthur. I got a postcard by the evening post from Arthur. It had been posted on the 28th of November and he seems well.

Today I met Stoffegan in the street and I hope to go to Woltershausen next week.

Belle has written me a note to the General Commander.

Saturday 5th December.

Sent a parcel to Arthur and had a visit from Miss Dora Marhgraf who promised to come and have a chat tomorrow. I also wrote to Emily.

Monday 7th December.

I had a long talk with Miss Marhgraf yesterday. She has just come from India and was in London on the 8th of November. She promised to visit the Plunketts for me. They are some Irish people I heard of who are in difficulties - a couple with a little child. I would go and visit them but I am not allowed out of Hildesheim.

I sent today a big box of cakes to Arthur from 'Lehans'.

Today they announce the fall of Lódz and the capture of two thousand Russians.

During the month of November the Germans took captive of eighty-five thousand Russians.

I visited the Police President and asked permission to go to Woltershausen. Rosie v.d. Busch went with me. We had a chat together and she said that there were over eight thousand soldiers yet in Hildesheim. Over forty-six thousand men have gone from here as soldiers. That means, of course, the men who have passed through the barracks.

There is a very fine regiment here – the 79 (Gibraltar) and it consists of twelve hundred men besides officers. These are regular men. The conscripts who have only served two years are not counted as regular soldiers. This fine regiment left here the first day of mobilisation and on the 1st of November. Three months after the war was declared. Not one man of that regiment who went out was still in the field. All were killed or wounded. Of course the regiment is constantly filled up by conscripts and they are all fine and willing. It is dreadful to think of it.

Tuesday 8th December.

I have just got permission to go to Woltershausen for a day.

Had a postcard direct from England from L. Lloyd and it has come right through and is stamped "Prisoner of War".

I also received a long letter from Emily Durselen and she speaks of taking the children to England in January. I feel nervous over their safety but they say the crossing is safe enough. A lot can happen before January.

I had a chat with a young lady today. She had a letter from the field from her brother and she read it to me. It was too sad. Of the three thousand men who went into battle the day Lódz fell only six hundred came back. The most of them were from here.

It is very distressing to go now in the streets and see the wounded. I cry every time I go out.

Every place is a lazarett - churches, picture galleries, dancing rooms, all big rooms in the hotels - and every hospital is cram full.

It is really dreadful to meet young men without both legs. Some have both eyes shot out and others have wounds innumerable. But the worst of all is the people who go mad. Some men go mad after being in battle and some wives go mad when they hear their husband has been killed. The asylum here is full up. Two came in last week, not at all wounded; only gone mad with what they had seen. What must it be like in the towns nearer the front? We are right inland and the worst cases cannot travel this far.

Wednesday 9th December.

I have been to see the children and poor people at the Krankenhaus. The children are fed each day at noon for a halfpenny each and the men and women for one penny. It is a splendid work. I got some books of tickets and they will be given to the poor children. People buy these tickets in books and give them to deserving cases. They are fed by the Nuns and it is splendid work.

We read today that the people say that the prisoners in Ruhleben are all well treated and they get plenty to eat and are comfortable. But they get no luxuries. I wonder what Arthur's opinion is.

Friday11thDecember.

Been today to the Gut at Woltershausen and every thing is well. Belle and I had a miserable walk but it cleared up after nine o'clock. Hermenia came to the station.

We heard that the Germans had lost four ships. We very seldom hear of a reverse so it rather astonished us.

Saturday 12th December.

I had a bad bout of neuralgia but sent the last box to Arthur. He had written during the week thanking me for the parcel from Belle. He never noticed it was from her and I am afraid he has got me into trouble with the police. All parcels from me must go through them. They will think I have sent one unknown to them.

Dr. Kahn also called and he says he has an allowance to go and visit Arthur. So in that case he goes to Berlin next week. I heard a lot today of the deceitful chatter in Woltershausen.

Sunday 13th December.

Been today to dinner with the Peligeaus and afterwards for coffee at Carole Osthaus'. We drew linen for the soldiers because wadding is scarce. The town is very full because people are here from the land to visit their men in the army. Two thousand more are to go away next week into Russia.

The Landstorm was called up last Thursday. Those born in 1876 and those being up to nineteen years old in that year must present themselves for military duty.

Wednesday 16th December.

I had a letter from Arthur thanking me for parcels.

Herr Pastor Gatsemire called this morning and I asked him to say two Masses for George (the coachman). It was so sad for he told me the account of his death after only eight days in the field.

Frau Gatsemire also came from Woltershausen and I had a long talk to her. She informed me that England had to answer for every drop of blood lost in this dreadful war.

Arthur writes me he has had a postcard from Belle and that his papers have left England.

We have had quite lovely spring weather. Until this day it has rained every day.

Today a lot of young men came in to commence their training. I met an officer this morning, a friend of v.d. Busch's and he is just recovering from shock. It's too sad to see him. He is a fine handsome officer of thirty-six-years-old and now he is just like a child in intellect. He was with eight officers, in a group, when the shot came and they all lay in pieces around him. He is not at all injured but keeps looking for his friends. I see him often as he passes here many times a day with his wife, mother and sister. His home is here.

The Hildesheim regiment 79 has had a deal of losses.

The news is very quiet this past eight days so I expect Germany is losing. Nothing is in the papers, only hate for England. I did hear that the Serbians had retaken Belgrade but it was not in the papers. Also that England has promised a lot of money to Portugal if she will go to war with Turkey. One has a deal to stand these days.

Thursday 17th December.

Hermenia came to see me and had dinner. We heard that the Germans had bombarded England, Scarborough and Hartlepool, with a loss of life of over one hundred killed and three hundred injured. Also that they have sunk two English undersea boats and that the flags are flying for the victory of Poland. It is reported that Poland is quite taken by the Germans and that the battle is a historical one with such a wonderful piece of generalship.

The school children have a holiday to celebrate the bombardment of England.

Sunday 20th December.

We heard of a great loss of English soldiers at Nieuport. Over six hundred lay dead in the field and one-thousand eight-hundred taken prisoner. The Germans report no losses.

The people are very busy getting ready for Christmas for the government has asked the people to make it as like Christmas as they can for the children. The shops are lovely. On Sunday they are opened from twelve o'clock in the morning until eight o'clock at night. So many people are here from the land and it is amusing, as well as sad, to see the people drive in. Many of them have a couple of milk cows instead of a horse. They collect their parcels and then drive off. Quite a lot of wagons were in the street and the cows were mooing all together.

Every house has sorrow. One girl I met today was going to visit her uncle for Christmas. He has had three sons killed in one week in France. Another was on a ship sent out to South Africa in October and never heard of since. All four sons are gone and all were between the age of twenty and twenty-eight.

I asked at the bank over the transfer of money to Holland for the children and Emily to get back to England. I was told the transfer is very high – ten for a hundred. I had better trust to changing little there.

I have been to pay a few calls but I am better at home. The people are so bitter against us.

Thursday 24th December.

I was able to go to confession. Belle knew a Dean of the Cathedral who could speak English and it was arranged for me to visit him.

We sent a parcel to the Plunketts in Hannover and one to Arthur in Ruhleben. Belle and I were very busy until quite late. I got an allowance from the police to stay out a little later than eight o'clock but I was not allowed to travel past the limit.

Christmas Day 1914.

I spent with Belle and Fraulein Vich. We had dinner and a cup of tea at the Marienhaus then went to see Fraulein Osthaus for supper.

Saturday 26th December.

Fraulein Osthaus, Belle and Fraulein Vich came to me for dinner and on Sunday Belle and I went to Frau v. Bruchausen to dinner. She had her daughter on a visit from Dresden and her husband has been in the field since the first week of the war. In the evening we went to Fraulein Vich and had some nice music.

Monday 28th December.

I received a letter from Hannover saying Mrs. Plunkett was going to England but not the Captain. Also one from California from Frank and he seems to have no idea of what the war means to us.

Wednesday 30th December.

I received a postcard from Arthur asking for a few things. I have sent twenty-five pounds to Emily for her journey and expect to hear she leaves today for England.

New Year's Eve.

We spent it as usual. Belle and I went for a walk in the morning - after my early visit to the police. We got a paper from America, which was just a month old, and it was a great pleasure. We went to the Dom for evening service and it was a very fine service. After church Carole Osthaus, Belle and I went to Marienhaus and had a glass of wine and a cake. I was home for ten o'clock.

New Year's Day 1915.

I dined at Peligeaus and we had a nice quiet time. I thank God that the holidays are over and I dare not even think of former Christmases and New Years.

Saturday 2nd January.

Belle and I heard of an English ship being wrecked, the **Formidable**, but the reports were confusing. One said a mine and one an undersea boat. Both stated that seven hundred lives were lost.

Belle wrote to Arthur and I went to the bank. They told me there that they had written to Herr Unquhart on November 26th telling him that there was no exchange of money between the two countries. Therefore he could have no cash sent to California until peace was declared.

Sunday 3rd January.

I had a visit from a Frau Gube. She is the daughter of an English professor and married to a German. Therefore she is not English. Her brother is in Ruhleben but he is to come home next week and go in the army having become naturalised.

I had notice today to get my photo ready for the 6th to take to the police as all must have them ready for the passports. The police have decided that we must each have one at once. I do not know for what reason.

We heard today that if the war lasts two months longer we shall have a famine.

I wonder why they do not write to me from home?

Monday 4th January.

I had a postcard from Emily saying herself and the children were in Köln on Saturday. Something over the passports to England I expect.

I also got a postcard from Arthur and he remarked that Herr Allorn was free (having naturalised) and he expected he had been to see me. And that I had received his message. Herr Allorn had not called here so Belle and I went to seek him. We never had such a cool reception. He told us nothing and said Arthur had only sent me greetings. He could not give us any idea of any further comforts we could send him and he never answered our questions ever. It is my opinion he has been jolly well frightened. Belle was very much astonished at our result. He goes directly into the army.

I had a visit from a lady here who is expecting her brother to become free. He goes directly into the army as soon as he is naturalised. He is thirty-four-years-old. She wishes he had stayed in Ruhleben. I am not sorry that Arthur is there now.

Today it has snowed all day and is still snowing even though it is late at night. If one had the heart to admire it then the Leden Strasse is a perfect treat. Every bush and tree is thick with snow and all the children with their sledges so merry. As a contrast we hear that Frau

Kor, who lives opposite this hotel, has died with heart failure on hearing her only son was wounded. She was working in her business a couple of hours before her death.

There is nothing but misery all around.

Arthur's last postcard was not all bright. I can see that he is very low spirited.

Tuesday 5th January.

Belle and I took a walk today to see the place under snow. It is really beautiful. The snow is quite eighteen inches thick. It has snowed without stop for thirty-eight hours and is still at it. It is not possible to describe the beauty of the place. The walk around the walls was simply perfect and many people were busy with their cameras. The snow plough had been all round and we had a path two yards wide banked each side with snow. The telephone lines are like thick ladders and there are so many broken. They hang like festoons everywhere and are thicker than a man's arm in snow. The fir trees are doubled over with the weight of the snow. Everywhere one hears the bells of the sleighs.

Each shopkeeper here keeps the snow runners ready for winter. They simply lift their everyday carriage or wagon from the wheels and place it on the runners. All the post vans, soldiers' carts, children's carriages etc. can be put on runners and you never see a pair of wheels. It seems so peaceful - the lovely white streets and the jingle of bells. Even the children's mail carts have bells.

The windows of my room are opposite the Wollenweber Strasse. It is a very old street of the 17th and 18th Century. The houses have very steep roofs, all kinds of gables, bay windows and little attics looking out of their deep mantle of snow and it is a perfect treat. Now and again we hear a rumble and hear the fall of snow from one or another of these roofs. But the houses have such deep overhangs that the snow clears the footway and falls directly into the street.

The soldiers make very merry and many a good game of snowballs I witness. The young girls and lads dare not throw snowballs at the soldiers when they are marching. They wait until they are under trees and the throw at the boughs so all the snow falls on them.

We saw a good joke this morning. Some girls did this trick, and when the front of the procession with the officer had turned a corner the four last soldiers in the procession pelted the girls awfully. A sergeant, who was walking in the streets, deliberately turned his back on them and stood looking at a fine garden as the girls got a good pelting. The soldiers then picked up their guns and ran after the procession and the people screamed with laughter. We left the sergeant admiring the garden scene. I admired him for his good sense. Those soldiers did so enjoy the two minutes on their own.

Some of these men are such nice fellows and I get quite used to them passing my window day after day, sometimes three times. I can single out faces and watch them each time. Then comes the day when they have the covered helmet and the corduroy trousers on. I see them no more. They have gone to the front.

I often cry when I miss them. But it is far worse when you see them a few weeks later in a bath chair and looking like death. One wonders how it is with his own people when it upsets a stranger so.

These days are too dreadful.

It is sad to go into the churches also – crowds of soldiers praying so fervently and during the Stations of the Cross. So many go away with the thought that they will not back come again.

The war seems wholesale murder. I hear so much I cannot write it.

The soldiers do not know when they leave here, or where they go to. The people do not know where they are until a letter comes to say. Many come back wounded a week later and many letters come home at the same time to say their last goodbye. A lady here got her first letter from her husband two weeks after his departure saying: 'Beloved wife, my last greetings on our third wedding anniversary'.

That was all he was able to write being mortally wounded. She was at home with a one-year-old baby.

I could tell scores of sad tales that happen here in Hildesheim. When a man is advertised as missing his people do not know if he is a prisoner in England, France or Russia. Or if it means he was blown to bits and cannot be identified.

When you send a parcel or letter you simply address it to so and so, such and such a regiment and the post forwards it to whichever country he is in.

Wednesday 6^{tth} January.

It is nine weeks since Arthur left here and there is no sign of him coming home at all.

Today rain has set in and the streets are dreadful with melting snow. There are no men to clean it and the telephone is quite at a standstill. So many wires are broken and so few men are left here to repair – all being at the front.

I have to take my photo to the police today.

Belle got a 'Times' (it was a perfect treat) of December 25th. It gave us such pleasure.

Thursday 7th January.

It is Belle's birthday so I went round to congratulate her. She had received a card from Arthur and a letter from Emily. The latter says they are on their way to Nijmegen (Netherlands) and the card was from Köln.

I had a visit also from Frau Grebe and her mother. She tells me that if her son gets away from Ruhleben then he must go to the front. He is thirty-five. Men up to forty-five are called up so I am glad Arthur is where he is.

It has rained all day and the snow is almost gone. One feels so sorry for the poor soldiers.

Tonight a three day preparation for a whole day of prayer commences. We go to a sermon in the cathedral for the first preparation tomorrow the 8th, which is a fast day. Saturday is a day of preparation and confession. Sunday is for communion and the offering up of the whole day in devotion all over Germany for peace. It is a grand idea with the whole country (Catholics) at one in prayer and fasting and Holy Communion for the one great cause. Let us hope there is soon a result.

Belle, Rosie and I went to the Dom early. There was a fine preacher and the place was packed. But the less said about the sermon the better. Of course, England was to blame for everything.

Friday 8th January.

We went to meet Frau v. d. Busch today it being her birthday. In the morning a policeman came here for my birth and marriage date etc. I got in a hobble when I went to the police for Arthur had not announced us when we came to stay here.

It appears that as soon as you come into a place to stay over a week you must go to the police of the place. You must give your age, place of birth, name etc. If you do not do so you are fined eight shillings. Of course they find you out if you stay longer. I suppose Arthur had more to think of. I asked if my man had not announced himself at the police, how was it that he was a prisoner. I thought we had been amused enough and said I thought the neglect lay upstairs with the police chief. I said that I could <u>not</u> understand them. I think they were glad to let me go. They were tired of hearing: 'I understand not'.

In the evening we went to the Dom to hear what the Father had to say but he was too ill to preach. I was not sorry for I enjoyed the sermon from a different priest far better.

Saturday 9th January.

When I visited Rosie v.d. Busch today I said how I had expected Arthur, after he had written, to come home. But she said I must not wish him free as all the men up to forty-five had been up for inspection. If he came out of Ruhleben it meant the front for him. I am so glad he is not here.

Things are very quiet and the people seem a little downhearted. They explain that the very wet weather we have had prevents them from going on. They are convinced that they are steadily winning. Still you can see that they are uneasy over no news. They commonly speak of Russia being finished before Christmas but we hear nothing at all from there.

Eight hundred men go away from here tonight. They do not know where and they will not be allowed to write home their address. They are allowed just the regiment and company and name. The letters will find them either in France, Belgium or Russia. Their people do not know where they fight in this bad weather as all the soldiers are given the same clothing.

Sunday 10th January.

It was a memorable day for me as regards church. I never saw so many communicants in one church before. It was the finish of the three days of prayer and all who could were to confess and communicate for the peaceful end of the war.

Another Father has come to preach at the Dom. It is really marvellous where the people come from. When you think that the place is only a third the size of Stockport it has eight Catholic churches. Also that more than half of the population is Protestant. Every church was full and you could not get near the confessionals. Priests came on the altar and said Mass and went off again. Still there were priests giving communion all the time at the altar rails. I heard three complete Masses and half a fourth. Still there were people waiting for communion.

Everyone goes to their church now for help. No one else can give them comfort. People who live in a free country do not have any idea of what war means in a conscript country. Misery is everywhere you go and each day buries more men.

I saw one of our young waiters at the church. He seemed full of trouble and afterwards I questioned him. He told me he has three brothers at the front - nineteen, twenty-one and twenty-two-years-old. His father was called up last Thursday. He is forty-five years old. He was very busy slaughtering, as he is a butcher, when the telegram came at noon. He went at once to the barracks, in his working clothes, and his wife ran to get help in the business to finish the slaughtering. At eight o'clock in the evening she got a telegram to say he was already in uniform and was in Munster. The poor boy said: 'My mother cannot cry any more. She has done so much. She can only pray for them all'.

If he was in England he would have no such trouble.

The head waiter told me today that everyone from nineteen to forty-eight years old must present themselves this month for an army of five million must be ready for April. So there is trouble for someone awaiting. It is such an anxious time and one hears such dreadful things.

Today I hear of twenty-four new Zeppelins for London. Each one is to carry fifty bombs of half a hundredweight each. They are going in nine weeks time and some of them are to be used in Nieuwpoort (Flanders) this week.

Got a postcard from Arthur and he wants a few things and a box to lock them in. It sounds as if someone is pinching. But I don't blame them if what I hear of the place is true.

Tuesday 12th January.

I saw many men come in. There was not one under forty years of age. I felt so sorry for them. They just tramped along with their cardboard boxes as if they noticed nothing. They were looking for the houses they were to sleep in. Everywhere is full up.

With fourteen-thousand soldiers in the place it makes a difference. Frau Kuhner is very ill, inflamation of the lungs, but they still have a soldier in quarters with them and it makes such a deal of work. One must be up to get his coffee before he goes out. The people never grumble and say they must do it for their country.

I feel so sad for the horses poor things. They seem so very strange in a town and prance about as if afraid. Their drivers, young boys, look sad over the affair and the masters ditto. Now there are no horses to do the heavy work and spring is coming.

Wednesday 13th January.

I have not heard anything of the war for nine days.

I had a letter from Emily yesterday. She is in Holland and writes that no one will change her German money. She is in a fix. I am so very sorry for her but she hopes to do better in Rotterdam. She says she has been to three banks but they will not change her any. I am anxiously waiting her next letter.

We hear of sixty flyers setting out for London. But the fog was so dense they could see nothing. On getting to Dover it was clear so they dropped a few bombs.

There are many new men in today and I hear we have fourteen-thousand men in the place. So you can guess that every home and place is full of them.

I was in the chemist's yesterday when a young man came in who was employed there and he was allowed to go free. There was great joy as the owner was at the front and he was the only capable one left - the rest being boys.

I have had a miserable two days, not busy at all, and my head nearly driving me frantic.

So many things are scarce though the prices are not high. It is just that things run out. Today it is posted that there will be no white bread after the 15th.

I was at the Peligeaus' today and they said that for many weeks no bird seed could be bought. Many people were letting the canaries fly out of their windows. Marie saw one a few days ago on the house tops. One came into their garden and they caught it. It was half dead with hunger. Having some seed from the last bird they had they fed it. It was over an hour in feeding. They will keep it as long as the seed lasts.

Thursday 14th January.

No war news today but we hear of a terrible earthquake in Italy and ten thousand are dead. Here they say it is a great punishment from God to the Italians because they have not kept their bond in the alliance. They have gone to war with the Russians rather than helping Germany.

Also had a letter from Emily in Holland. She says she is waiting there for the birth certificates of the children which must come from England before they can be allowed on board ship. She has had a very rough time with the journey. I am glad I did not ask her to take the children. Now that it has turned out to be such a bad journey it's perhaps as well that she suggested it herself.

I am very anxious over them. In fact the anxiety is making me quite ill. As the letters are three days old before I get them it is very likely she is on her journey home by this time. She has heard how very badly the Germans are treated in England and seems anxious over her reception.

Well, she can't be any worse treated than I am here. In fact it will take a great deal to make me believe that the English so far forget themselves. She writes that her opinion has changed since she left here. She hears more news but cannot tell it to me. I wonder over it often.

Today the death is announced of the young priest who preached the sermon in the cathedral on Thursday last which so much surprised me. I think the poor man must have been partly delirious when he spoke to us that night. He was taken to the hospital on the Friday and was high in fever (Scarlet). He just sank and died on the Wednesday evening following. It's a very sad case as he is only thirty-two-years-old and was a marvellous preacher.

There is a lot in the papers at present of what Father Vaughn has been saying. The Jesuits here greatly deplore his sermon. I should like to read it. The Jesuits also remark that he did <u>not</u> say all that was published in the papers here as regards the Kaiser. We have written to a friend for a book of the sermon from England.

Today is miserable and I have been ill all day.

Friday 15th January.

This morning I was awakened by the noise of many horses in the streets. They were for the front and were principally working horses for all the good ones went away early in the war. These were left for the farmers to use in the fields but now even these are going and they are here for examination. Some of these are poor enough and seem to me to be aged also.

Saturday 16th January.

Today is the last muster of horses and some fine heavy ones are in the town. I hear that two thousand soldiers leave here along with the horses in the next few days. From Monday the whole of the railway is held up for the transport of troops and horses. From the provence (that is ours) nine thousand men and a great many horse are to go. It is what they call the second muster and it will occupy the rail for five days. So no railway travelling for anyone else. Also the second Landstorm is called up. That is all up to forty-five years old. If Arthur was free he would have to go to the front.

We hear today of a great German victory in Flanders by Soissons. They have captured four thousand five hundred Frenchmen and as many guns. It seems to be a great advantage. We have no news of Poland for over a week.

I had a visit from Dr. Kahn today. He has been to Ruhleben to see Arthur and says he looks very well. I am so glad to hear it. He has brought me a paper giving me the control of the whole estate.

It is a comfort to hear someone say that they think that the war will be over by Easter and most people think June or July. But one man today said it cannot last longer than Easter really. I do some times lose all hope of better times.

Sunday 17th January.

Today the streets are full of soldiers for they commence to go away tomorrow, also the horses. Over two thousand men in all to go from here and six hundred horses. But where to? They themselves do not know.

There are notices in the papers telling us to be careful of white bread and tea. The flour will have to last out until we have new wheat.

They are collecting old woollen clothes at all the houses. These are then are made into under-woollens for the soldiers and the pieces left over are joined up into patchwork rugs for the men. They are also asking you to sell all old silver spoons, ornaments etc. And are giving you the address to take it to.

Whole houses of people give their time to sewing all day for the army and are making all kind of things. I think all things on sale for the field are dear of course. They are considered as luxuries. I bought half-a-pound of butter in a tin for a shilling and two pence and I thought it dear.

Also the cardboard boxes are so expensive. I send one to Arthur about six inches deep, twenty inches long and twelve inches wide and it cost four pence. It makes parcels dear for poor people. Petroleum is very scarce. Forty-five pfennigs a quart. That is five-pence-halfpenny English and you cannot get it at that. No shopkeeper dare sell to any one person more than half a quart.

I had a postcard from Emily today, it has been five days coming, and she hopes to sail on Saturday the 16th for home.

Tuesday 19th January.

Belle sent a parcel to Arthur today and he writes me there are several things they are not allowed to have now. Chocolate, cakes jams etc. They are getting scarce.

We have now been warned for a long time about the white flour.

There came a sudden order today for Russia. Over a thousand soldiers left here at five o'clock and they had no idea, at noon, they were to go. The organisation of the men is really marvellous. This is the first time for many weeks that they have been told where they are to go.

I was at the baths yesterday and saw the people fetching their coke. There were six or eight women pulling a cart that ought to have a horse. The cart contained twenty or thirty bags of coke on it and at the back were a dozen women pushing.

So many poor people with baby carts are getting a hundred weight or so of coke. There are no men to hawk the coke and no horses to take it in the streets. The people must get it themselves. Now and then I would pass a handcart being pushed by a soldier. Very likely the house he was lodging at had no fire.

What struck me most was the silence of them. Not a word was spoken as the procession of little and big carts passed up the street. The cokes are only given or sold at a certain hour and the streets are full for a time. Even in the cases where six or eight girls or boys were with a cart there was no noise. Everyone here seems full of grim sorrow but they are confident of victory. Even in the churches. When the Bishop's letter was read for New Year he asked us all not to be too proud of when the news of the victory came and the Germans were the noble conquerors.

Thursday 21ˢᵗ January.

We read of the airship being over Yarmouth and Cromer. They say here that over two hundred are killed and many wounded. They are very delighted about the damage to a military school and stocks.

Friday 22nd January.

We have no news at all only a lot about the Yarmouth damage. But there is something in the papers over Romania and Italy which does not seem to please them.

I am very anxious over Emily and the children and expect a card each post.

The papers today tell us that the result of collecting old woollens from house to house, to make up for the soldiers, has proved to be very successful. They are now going to have a collection from house to house of old metal of any kind. So if we have any old silver or bronze ornaments etc. we must give them up. There was an advertisment in the papers a few weeks ago telling you where to take all old silver and it would be bought from you. Candlesticks, spoons, jewellery etc., anything at all out of silver. Now it is all kinds of metals.

Saturday 23rd January 1915.

Today they tell us in the papers that all pigs must be killed off because the food is scarce. The flesh must be made into sausages or be put in tins for future use. There is not enough food for the animals so they are killing off all they can. Especially all those we can cure and keep. So many things are scarce. One has a fear for a famine.

A number of soldiers go away again today. It really is a wonder where all the men come from but this lot are particulary sad. They are the men who are home after being wounded and were in the surrounding villages getting stronger – mostly with their parents and wives. They had been told they could rest until Easter but they got twenty-four hours notice to go to the Doctor. Then they were off to the front. I felt so sorry for them for it was to Russia they went. It's so very cold there besides the food being scarce.

We hear in the papers that after the next term the Turkish language is to be taught in the German schools instead of English. The hatred is dreadful and we must not speak a word of English in the streets. Two ladies in Hannover were mobbed because they were heard to speak English. We saw a motto in a window last week - 'God punish the Englishman'. That is the universal greeting instead of – 'Good day'. These are dreadful days to live through. I did not think that human beings could live and show so much hate.

Sunday 24th January.

The papers are full of the scarcity of food today and tell us we shall have to eat bread made of barley. They must have the oats for the horses.

We have had a slight frost for four days and I could think that the forest looks lovely. But I am not allowed to go so far. I am only allowed just over two miles and the finest parts are quite three miles distant. I am sure that the trees covered with the hoar frost are beautiful.

It is quite confirmed today that we are prepared for a scarcity of food and other supplies. Fresh meat is getting scarcer but the price remains the same as before. Cocoa, tea, chocolate, flour, oil candles, leather, meal and rubber have been scarce for some time.

It was announced in church today that on the Kaiser's birthday next Wednesday that there will be High

Mass also. The collections on Wednesday and next Sunday are for a birthday offering for the Kaiser to use as he thinks fit.

Monday 25th January.

We hear today of the whole coast of England being surrounded by undersea boats and nothing can come in or out. Also that the cruiser Blucher has been sunk in a battle at sea. Herr Roeder's brother was an officer on that and there is great distress in the hotel today. He was here for Christmas. We hear also that a large English ship has been sunk by a German mine but I have not heard the name of it.

Today I had a call from Frau Baroni and she tells me she had seventeen relatives in the war. Two are dead; three are prisoners, and the others still in the war. So she has anxiety. Her only son is in training for an officer. She asked me to go and live with her.

I went this morning to help with the hot milk for the poor Catholic children at the folk school or board school. We gave about one and a half gills of hot milk to each child and they brought their own bread and lard. I was very astonished to find the one hundred and sixty children were all boys. Of course I asked where the girls were. The answer was: 'We must look after our boys first. They are our future soldiers'.

I asked: "And aren't your girls the future mothers of soldiers?"

But there was no reply. If that is not enough to breed a German Mrs. Pankhurst I don't know what is. Being in a strange land I did not say much. I felt very indignant for I think the idea is to breed selfishness in the men. The German man is selfish enough.

Tuesday 26th January.

Today I went to Woltershausen with Herr Mumers. I only wanted seven hours leave from Hildesheim and had to wait six days to obtain it. We got our papers all right and the day was beautiful. I could not say how very beautiful the place was. Herr Mumers says it is much more beautiful in the winter than the summer. Everything was covered with three or four inches of snow and it really was a picture. Our house looked lovely. All the trees round it were thickly covered with snow and the bushes were quite as big again. The pond was frozen over and it looked so very nice. We had a treat of a day.

Steinoff tells us that he has received notice to kill or sell so many pigs. He has to give up to the government all food stuffs – grain, potatoes, straw, hay – being only allowed to keep fifty pounds of wheat for each person in the household and food for a few pigs. The others must be killed to save food. Also no bakehouse dare bake white bread of any kind and no household must do ditto. Everyone is liable to a severe penalty. So much barley or potato must be put with it. The soldiers' bread is all rye flour.

The Germans ridicule the idea that Germany lost The **Blucher** and England no boat. They say they distinctly saw one go down but could not see her name. They say that the reports extracted from the English papers say that the English did not lose any. The German papers question it.

Wednesday 27th January.

It is the Kaiser's birthday and there is great rejoicing here. All the flags are out in all the churches and it is a general holiday. The poor boys only got their milk.

Thursday 28th January.

We hear of a German victory over the French with a number of French and English killed and wounded.

I was speaking this morning to a schoolmaster. His son is at home for a few days, not being well. He was by Arras and has told his father that the orders these past few weeks were to show no mercy to the English. This was because the latter on one occasion had shown the white flag. When the Germans went towards them they fired on them. So since then no mercy is to be shown to the English.

We have, every Sunday, lectures on the English and it closes with songs and recitations on the hatred of England. I remarked last week that they should change The Lord's Prayer at once and pray 'Forgive us our trespasses but punish all who trespass against us'. The hatred is unbelievable. I shall be afraid to be here if such a thing happened that England won a battle.

They say here that it was a mere nothing on Sunday last but the quotations from English papers read different. We cannot get to know the name of the English ship that is supposed to be lost.

Friday 29th January.

We read today that the boat lost last Sunday was the **Lion**. They do not say how many lives were lost. They also remark that two torpedo boats of the English were sunk.

There is announced today the loss of an airship (Zeppelin) in Russia. The men were saved but imprisoned. We also hear that the Germans have made headway in France.

I went to see Grebe the agent for the estate today. He says the war will last another twelve months.

Saturday 30th January.

No news today, only that of the seven flyers (French) three were shot down by the Germans and a famous flyer was killed.

I went a little way on my own today in the forest for it was so very beautiful. We have had this frost nearly a week and everything is lightly covered with snow. They are tobogganing on Galgen (gallows) Hill and it is a lovely sight. The trees have a covering of ice on all the branches and just look like huge glass chandeliers with the sun shining through them. Some of the icicles hanging down from the trees are half a yard long. When a slight wind comes they ring as they touch one another and then fall to the ground. I have never seen anything like it. Not even on the stage.

I stood half an hour watching the young people with their sledges. The view was magnificent off the hill and for miles and miles nothing but snow. Then I saw a long black line just like a snake. It was the soldiers going to the shooting range and the others coming back. In the distance there was the constant shooting where the men were learning to shoot human beings. Perhaps some of them, before two days older, would be dead themselves. To my back was the lovely forest and over all there was such a beautiful blue sky and brilliant sunshine. One could not believe that a war was raging and that a thousand of these soldiers are going away tonight.

Sunday 31st January.

We hear today of ten thousand Russians being captured. It's a very large amount. This week they have given the amount of prisoners they have in Germany. It is enormous.

Russian officers 3,575 – men 506,294 – Generals 18.
French officers 3,459 – men 215,905 – Generals 7.
Belgian officers 612 - men 36, 825.
English officers 492 - men 18,824.

Rye bread has risen in price and is two pence a pound. When one remembers it is not as nutritious as white bread you think it dear. White bread is sold by the small dinner cob, not by weight at all.

Steinoff writes me he has sold the fowls. He could not buy food for them.

Monday 1st February 1915.

I hear this morning that the German undersea boats have sunk three steamers. Two near Liverpool and one near Le Havre but the men were saved. They were trading vessels taking food into England.

Went to the bank and sent the money to Königswinter and to Lamspringe but find I have other rates to attend to.

I hear that Herr Allorn who was in Ruhleben with Arthur has gone to the mad house. He first went to Hannover to go in the army but his complaint grew much worse and he is now put away. I thought him queer when I last visited him.

Tuesday & Wednesday 2nd & 3rd February.

There is nothing to report. The Kaiser has gone to Poland. The Russians have been making headway. The Germans are glad one of the boats sank because it had so much food on it and because it was going to Belgium.

I went out to tea today and we talked of the shortage of supplies. They fear a famine and we are told that there will be a shortage of meat after this week.

A letter has been received from a doctor from this town who is in Russia. He must be out of the regular track of the war as he asks for supplies. He says he is in a dreadful fix and has to take the shirts off the men to tear into bandages. They have no beds or necessaries and he must put the men, partly naked, in straw on the floor and the men are constantly dying off. His letter was very dreadful to read. I did thank God that none of mine were in the war in Russia.

Wichman, the electrician from Lamspringe, came to see me today. He is an under officer here and trains the men. He tells me this last lot are all Landstorm and many are forty-two and forty-five years old. Some of them have never been in the army before. They were not accepted because of their eyes or other ailments. Now all must go up and it's so very difficult to drill them. Many often have five and six children and some of them have sons in the army. He says the work is hard.

Women are now to do men's work and they have women as porters, signalmen, ticket collectors etc. They also work in the post office and in the town as snow shifters. There is no one else to do it.

During February and after there is to be no more white bread. <u>War bread</u> is to be baked made from oats, rye, potatoes and barley and all people must eat it. If a baker is caught baking any white bread, even for his own family, he is subject to a severe penalty.

Most of the Schnapps breweries have been closed for some time for they dare not buy potatoes or corn for the schnapps. In fact all luxuries are forbidden. Of course we can do without drink if we could get the food. The beer is still there but the breweries are short of men. The hotels are feeling the shortage of food and I cannot buy many little things myself. People are not allowed to buy large quantities of food as it all must be evenly distributed.

Hermenia came from Woltershausen and she says all is well there. Several men have returned cripples and one will not get better. She says all the corn and potatoes have gone to the army. The farmer is only allowed enough to seed his land and fifty pounds for each person in his house. So regards horses this is bad as he is only allowed to feed them with two pounds of corn a day. The rest must be straw or chaffs. No horse can work on that. Our 'Moor' used to get fourteen pounds a day and all other horses got ten to twelve pounds. I feel so sorry for them.

We read of the coal strike in England and it gives the Germans great pleasure. They say that the English people are quite sick of English laws and that they do not know how to govern workers.

Belle has told me of the intention of Germany to block all the neutral waters and shipping. They say here that the neutral lands are sick and tired of being dictated to by England, who rules the waves, and are glad another power has stepped in to show her her place. I myself cannot see the neutral lands quietly sitting down to that. We are told that after this blockade begins on the 18th of February the war is only a very short time to the finish. I wonder what England thinks of it.

There is a very strange article in the papers. I believe it is to the effect that England has decided to fly neutral flags on all her ships to repay Germany for what she intends doing regarding the blockade. The papers here say that it is the Admiralty's orders. I flatly said I did not believe that. For if it was so, and allowed, then why had not Germany or England done it before. Also that this was not allowed at sea and I did not think that even if England could see herself being beaten she would play a false game. She was too sportsmanlike for that.

We hear nothing from anywhere only from the German bureau and no news of the enemy. Only that each day they are sent further back. Where to? They do not say. It's my opinion these things are only put in the papers to take the people's thoughts off the war because there is no definite news

Yesterday there was the weekly lecture on the war and the hatred of England. The people were told that it is not German man against English man but also German woman against English woman. The women of Germany must remember that. I wonder if ever there will be a revolution here and the people will use these words again. It is not a pleasant time to live in. Thank God there are a few of nature's women left but yet there are so very few. In some things one hears you can fancy you are among people of the early ages. Perhaps these are reborn again and are from the time of the Barbarians. Surely never before in the age of Christianity have the people said such things that we hear today.

Sunday 7th February.

A great day all over Europe for peace – in the Catholic churches of course. I do not hear much of the Protestant.

I hear today from a lady that she had a letter from a nephew in England, a German, and he says that only two thirds of the Germans are prisoners and that the remainder are free. I wonder if this is true. At the time of Arthur's arrest the papers here said that even people up to sixty years of age were imprisoned in England and that their wives and children were in dreadful poverty.

Monday 8th February.

Today the papers announce they have lost a few shooting graves in France. This is the first time they have announced their losses. They also say that a terrible battle is raging in Poland. A battle the like of which the world has never been seen before. There are so many people in it. I forget how many Germans are there but it is enormous.

We hear there is a great to-do about coal in England for their use. They must mean a strike.

The Socialists have had a meeting and say the war must go on to the bitter end. Here they are confident of victory and we are anxiously awaiting the 18th.

Tuesday 9th February.

There is serious news today from the baker here. You can only get bread from the baker as no one else sells it. We are informed that after the 12th of this month only so much per person is to be allowed. Each person gets a paper from her baker and she has to write how many people she requires bread for and she is told how much per day she can have and no more. It is to make the people eat more potatoes because they fear a famine in corn and they must have what oats there are for the horses. Indian corn or maize we have not had since September.

Two thousand eight hundred men leave here today for Russia. Hindenberg, the General, says that they must take Warsaw at any cost of men and ammunition before the 18th.

Such a lot of Landstorm are called up. Poor fellows, I do feel sorry for them. They look bewildered. It seems that the Landstorm up to forty-five years old that had already done their military duty were called up at the end of November.

The same aged men who for some reason or other had not done military duty were left until later. These are the men we see now. Many of them have scarcely seen a town. They are from far in the country and you can tell that by their clothing. They stop everywhere in the street to ask where is the address they must go to, for they know nothing of the place. Their language is <u>so broad</u> as we say, ('platt' here), that many of the people do not understand them. It is much more pitiful in a strapping man of forty-five than in a raw country lad of twenty.

Today is just like spring. I went down by the river for a walk and heard such a lot of crows crowing and they were so busy building their nests. I sat down to watch them. It reminded me so much of the days I used to walk to Northenden to visit Mary Chandler. I used to stop and watch the crows there with little Winnie.

Wednesday 10th February.

Our men have gone to Russia. I heard them passing the hotel this morning at a quarter to five. People are up in this place at four o'clock. The soldiers went down in their twos and threes just like our men (English) going to the mills in the morning. And never a word was spoken.

They all lined up outside the station. I got up to see a few hundred pass here. There is never any rejoicing or playing of music here over the war. The Kaiser said no music was to be played or cheering done until they came home victorious.

Today we elected our new Bishop of Hildesheim. The late one was made Prince Bishop of Breslau in November and I went to the Dom for the ceremony. It took two-and-a-half hours but it was worth it. The service was very fine but we are all so weary.

Belle and I talk over what we read in the papers. It seems as if after the 18th there will be a long account of catastrophes around England.

I think of my homeland very, very often.

Still no news from Russia and they have been fighting for three days. But there is something in the papers about England flying the stars and stripes and playing a dirty game.

Thursday 11th February.

It always seems to me that when they have no war news that they fill the papers up with hate of England and what they will do to her.

Today is examinations at the schools and it seems so strange to see soldiers going to school. These are the young men who were studying at the schools for lawyers, solicitors or civil service and have been called up to their army service. They are allowed to return these last three days for their examinations. They return to the military directly the school is over.

Dr. Kahn called on his way home from Hannover and he has been to see a few prospective tenants for the house. I am to go next week for three days and see one or two of them. I shall be glad to settle it all.

The result of the collecting of woollen goods was announced yesterday. After making up hundreds of useful clothing and rugs for the soldiers the woollen rags that they could not use up, parings etc. were sold for five-thousand shillings for the Red Cross Society. That was here in Hildesheim and the same thing was all over Germany in the large towns. I wonder what the metal week will bring them.

Uncle George Steffen is at the front. He is forty-five and after a month of drilling he was sent away. I am so very sorry. It grieved me to hear of him going away. He was so kind to us all.

We have the baker's report today. Each person cannot have more than three-and-a-half pounds of bread per week. I thought it was a mistake and that they meant per <u>day.</u> But it is per <u>week!</u> The rest must be potatoes. Nice isn't it? I was very much astonished because we have always been told we had food enough for three years. Now they say it is because they have so many captives to feed. I remarked: 'But what of the men we have less - dead and captured Germans?'

Apparently these are very few.

Friday 12th February.

I have received today a letter and a postcard from James Walmsley in Blackpool. The pleasure was so great that I cried with joy. It's the first letter from England since September that I have received. I cannot write of the pleasure it gave me. James writes that things are normal there. I wish they were here. But he says it will be a very long time before we have peace.

Thank God all are well. That's something to know.

Just received a postcard from Arthur and he is well and has the hope of returning. He says all the landowners (German) in England are now free and he hopes things to be the same in Germany. It's good news.

Saturday 13th February.

A Russian downfall is reported today. Twenty-six thousand captured by the Germans. The news is especially welcome for there has been none for some time. All the flags are out. They say that in a few days we shall be in Warsaw.

There is a great deal in the papers today of the strong measures England is to take with the foreigner. I always feel alarmed when I read it. It always falls on us, the foreigners, here.

I went to see Grebe today and he will arrange to help me with the removing. Dr, Kahn says he has let the place. I go on Monday for a few days.

Monday 15th February.

I heard an officer say today that if half the powder used by the English and French had been good then all the Germans would be dead. He says of every ten hand bombs thrown in their shooting graves (trenches) only two are good and eight never explode. It's been the same all through the war.

We hear today that in England the Suffragettes have got two regiments ready. They make great fun of it here for they have always ridiculed the Suffragettes.

Annie (Drummond) Dröege
1874 - 1940

Arthur Joseph Dröege
1871 - 1950

and when the 136 Germans went towards
them. they fired on them. So since
then. no mercy is to be shown to the
English. We have every sunday lectures
on the English. & it closes with songs
& recitations on the Hatred of England.
I remarked last week. that they had
better change the Lords Prayer at once
and pray. Forgive us our trespasses. but
punish all who trespasses against us.
The Hatred is unbelievable, I shall be
afraid to be here if such a thing
happened that England won a battle,
They say here that that was a mere
nothing on Sunday last. but the
quotations from English papers read
different & we cannot get to know
the name of the English ship, that
is supposed to be lost.
Friday. 29th. We read to day that the
boat England lost last Sunday was the
Lion but they do not say how many lives
were lost. Also they remark 2 torpedo

28th & 29th January 1915.
Annie details German hatred for the enemy.

Annie and Winnie 1913

John Drummond with his eight children 1912

l - r back   Jim ... Kitty ... Gertrude's husband ... Will's wife
l - r middle Esther ... Jack .... Will ... George ... Gertrude
l - r front   Arthur Droëge ... John Drummond ... Annie

Annie and 'Uncle' George at the Roder-hof
4.8.1913

Annie, Arthur and Winnie in the Kloister Wald
6.8.1913

Annie, Arthur & 'Moor'

Tuesday 16th February.

We hear of a great German victory in Russia by Königsberg and now there are no more Russians in Germany. She is free of the enemy and all have been driven to their own land again.

Wednesday 17th February.

Great rejoicing over yesterday's battle and bands are playing. The results are published. Fifty thousand prisoners alive, many thousands have been killed, one hundred and ten large guns and large stores of clothes and food stuffs.

We have received a paper from London today and it is of the 30th of January. We are very much surprised to read that the Germans are not in Soissons. Here they say they are and have been since January 15th. One scarcely knows what to believe.

Thursday 18th February.

We are almost afraid to read the telegrams today for the papers are sure of a great sea battle. They say that yesterday they sunk three ships, one coal boat, and two food and goods ships and also that a large English man-of-war is injured. We scarcely know what to think, or whether to believe it.

The bread is <u>awful.</u> I heard at school today that the teachers have to go to all houses and see how much foodstuffs the parents have in hand.

We read today that in Russia the government has taken from the Germans all their food and land. Severe steps are to be taken here. I wonder if it will affect <u>us</u> in any way. One never knows.

The shoemaker told me today that all the hides of animals had to be sent directly to the government for leather and that he could not get any. He said it was not half tanned before it was used and could not last long. They are so short of pairs of men's boots that cost twenty-two shillings before the war that they are now thirty-five shillings.

Friday 19th February.

We hear today that in Belgium the French have suffered severe losses. We also hear that the Germans have lost two Zeppelins through the machines going wrong in a storm. All the men were saved but two.

The school where I go to give out the milk has to send half their scholars home at half time for they have no teachers. Out of a staff of twelve only three remain. <u>I mean men of course.</u>

Saturday 20th February.

We hear a lot today of the Russian losses. They have a lot of spoil here in Germany and say that the Russians left behind a box of gold with half-a-million gold pieces in it.

I hope to go to Woltershausen tomorrow. I have had such a deal of worry that I have given all to the lawyer and Herr Grebe to do.

As I came from the police today I saw about thirty Poles (Russian) being taken to the police office with an escort of six policemen. I made enquiries and heard that they are Russian Poles and had left one farm and gone to another to work. They had not asked the police. It will mean either a few days imprisonment or a pretty stiff fine. It's an awful place to live in. If I went out of here for a few hours I should be the same.

I heard yesterday that if I go to the lawyer for advice then he is bound to report my visit and any business to the police under a severe penalty. <u>Nice isn't it?</u>

Sunday 21st February.

We got two telegrams saying that China and Japan are going to war and that the Germans have sunk an English troopship with two-thousand men on board. They also report they have sunk a second ship but no details are to hand.

There is a special Thanksgiving Day by order of the Kaiser in all churches, Protestant and Catholic. In Germany they declare 'God is with us' after each day of devotion in the churches when they have had a victory. We had our last on February 7th and on the 14th a great fight took place. It was the same after the three days of devotion in December.

Monday - Wednesday 22nd - 24th February.

I was in Woltershausen. On my return I heard of the loss of two thousand men in England (cannot be true). I read in a weekly paper that the French are in Soissons, not the Germans, though we have had a rejoicing here for that victory.

The reported German gains in the last victory in Russia is over one hundred thousand men captive, many dead, seven Generals, one hundred and fifty cannons, one hundred and fifty ammunition wagons, three Red Cross wagons and a deal of clothing and food, also gold. The last I do not believe as people do not take gold on the battlefield. I also doubt the numbers. The people here believe every number.

I have a map but cannot follow the war for the reports are so confusing.

I had a very busy time at the house in Woltershausen and I sold a great deal of furniture and am glad all is away now. I could fill pages of this book with my experiences but that is not war items.

The bread here is awful and so many people are ill. It's a treat to get a bit of bread you can eat. Yet they tell us we have enough for three years. I fail to see that. The bakers dare not sell you any yeast and prevent the people baking at home and so having more than three-and-a-half pounds of bread per week. If you have a visitor then you must go to the police and give their name and address and you get a card to purchase another three-and-a-half pounds of bread for your guest. All common tea and coffee is sold out and now there is only the best at the price of four shillings for a pound of tea and two shillings and sixpence for coffee. The people are roasting rye and grinding it for coffee.

So many things are scarce that one fears a famine. They say, 'No, we can last three years'.

Arthur writes me that he will not get free. I never expected it.

Thursday 25th February.

Two thousand men left here for Russia. I think that Germany has had many losses. It's very sad to see the men going away in crowds and one can scarcely realise the numbers that go from here.

We have read that a regiment of Suffragettes has landed in Le Havre, the French coast, and are to take duties as chauffeurs, telegraphers etc. in the field. I was glad to read it for it shows that the English women are not all talk.

Friday & Saturday 26th & 27th February.

We hear of a few thousand more Russians being prisoners. But we get that news everyday. They also tell us that seven English ships have been sunk and that the Americans are making a deal of fuss over a ship of theirs, the **Evelyn,** which sank either on a mine or by torpedo boat. The Germans say it was a mine.

There is a long article in the papers about a great discovery a chemist has made. He can grind straw so fine that we can use it as flour and it has great nutriment. So we are likely to have straw bread now.

Sunday 28th February.

We read for the first time that the English are bombarding the Dardanelles and it seems like old news. They say that they have taken the first forts and have cleared the sea for four miles of bombs and mines.

For the past few weeks here the wounded officers have been very busy in the schools. Every boy from sixteen years of age must present himself (or pay a large fine) at a certain school twice a week for drill. It lasts for three hours each time and they are drilled just like soldiers. One day they were taken into the drilling field and taught shooting lying on the ground. They came home such dirty sights. It goes on each week and they <u>must</u> go to the practice.

Monday 1st March 1915.

I got a notice from the police today that I must go and take three photographs and any means of identification I have such as papers. They are giving us our passports. One photo goes to Berlin, one to Hannover and one here. I have one which I took to the police on January 7th on my pass. They seem rather uneasy over the Americans here but still have no fear of losing.

Tuesday 2nd March.

We have announced today a collection for gold from house to house. Anyone found keeping a store in the house will be severely punished. I have not seen any gold since August.

I hear also that the Red Cross Society is in a low condition. It will be dreadful if that has no funds as so many people rely on it for food.

Today I got a letter from dad posted on the 8th February and all is well at home, thank God. He writes me that Kittie is engaged to be married. I do hope that all is well with her. But she has Joyce close by. It does seem strange to think of her married. James and Kittie were the two babies and it makes me feel so old. Ettie also sent me a note. She says that baby Joan is just like a beautiful doll. I do long to see them all and to read of the Canadian news. I have not heard of our Kittie since she wrote off the boat and I often feel uneasy. I think of her scores of times a day. We were together for a week. It was the first week in March last year. All on our own and I stayed with her in Stockport. It is a pleasant memory now. One does not value those days until one has a time like this.

It is now eighteen weeks since Arthur left me here alone and it is like eighteen months. What must it be like for him? I sent him a parcel today and he tells me they are not allowed to write so often now. I shall only get a postcard or one letter a week.

I had a long chat with the agent today, Grebe and he told me that Germany had lost one million men. He said the war would last certainly another twelve months. If it was over next August, he said, that would be the soonest. It makes me feel ill to think of it. I do not think, myself, it can hold out so long for so many things are failing.

There is a notice in the papers today saying that no fat of any description must be used in the making of soap as it all must be used for foodstuffs. The notice also asked the people to limit their food for the new potatoes will not be ready before July. I think they fear a famine and the begging of gold this last two months has been each day. Banks and shops give you an extra six pence if you give them gold, i.e. sixpence on one pound sterling.

I heard today of an artist, English and lived in Goslar, who is now in Ruhleben. His wife and child are reduced to want. I wish I knew them. A lady here told me of them and said that a few German ladies sent her a few shillings a week to live on and that she went out cooking and sewing. She will not be able to send her husband any luxuries. I mentioned him to Arthur and I hope he finds him. But there are so many in Ruhleben.

It is very bad to go in a place of business as the regular men are at the front and the new ones are strangers to the trade. In our hotel we have six waiters, a boots, and a coachman and all have been changed four times with the exception of the head waiter and one young one. When one goes into the army we get another and in a few weeks he goes away. And so on. The head waiter is in delicate health, also the young one. That is why we keep them.

The Proprietor, Herr Roeder, has been called up twice but has managed to return. So many businesses have been closed because the proprietors are at the front. In Hamburg the state has had to appoint a manager for many an English works. The owners are prisoners and there is no one left to work the business. I met a Mr. Prahl, a relation of ours, he was in England for four years and he has a business (shipping) in Hamburg. He has not turned over a penny since August 10th and his capital is in England and he can get none. He is in a fix. He prophesies many a bankruptcy after the war is settled. I feel so sorry for him.

Wednesday 3rd March.

It is ridiculed here that the Turks have lost four forts at Constantinople - 'Another English lie'

Now our bread is weighed out to us. I would not care how little we got if only it was good. Each person gets half-a-pound of bread per day and no more. Not white bread, just the German rye bread and it is mixed with potatoes etc. It is very heavy to digest.

Thursday 4th March.

We got an English paper of the 18th of February and were delighted by it. We read that the Americans are for England. At this date here they say all the American sympathy is for Germany. Again we do not know what too believe.

Friday 5th March.

There is great laughter here. They tell us in the papers that the 4th March was a great day for them. The stupid foes made such blunders. Firstly, an English ship, full of guns and ammunition, was crossing to France but before the men would sail they had to make them drunk. The consequence was that they lost their way and landed their ship in Ostend. It sailed right into the enemies' hands. Secondly, the French mistook a convoy of French prisoners for German troops and fired on them killing them all. So they killed their own men. Never can they forget this March 4th for the laughter it caused them. They freely state this in the papers. The people believe that the English soldiers have refused to cross the Channel as they are afraid of the undersea boats. Therefore the fall of Paris is not a long time off for there is a shortage of soldiers.

Many thousands of German soldiers are being sent to Constantinople on Saturday for the defence. They are to travel overland so there must be some truth in what they say about the bombardment of the Dardanelles though it is, to a certain extent, denied here.

Saturday 6th March.

We have a telegram today saying an undersea boat, the "U8", has been sunk by an English torpedo boat. But the Germans must remember that they have taken twenty-eight English and French ships since the blockade of the 18th began.

Things are pretty scarce here and there is an announcement in the papers saying there will be no bread sold for three days. Also that from the morning of the first day no one can lay in a store.

The clothing for soldiers is running short and they are wearing such dirty patched clothes which I have never seen before. All are different coloured overcoats with the numbers on the arms. Green, black, blue, brown, all the colours of the rainbow and of course it is not as good a cloth as the general military cloth. It's a blessing the worst of the winter is over for the poor soldier's sake, especially if we are so short of wool.

Sunday 7th March.

Our Kittie's birthday - I wonder how she is and if she and Joyce are together.

During Lent here there are special sermons on the war by order of the Kaiser and the churches are full. There are confessions every morning during Lent from six o'clock until seven-thirty and in the evening from six till nine. Sunday morning included.

A very strange affair occurred by this hotel on Friday and just five hundred yards from our door. A taxi was coming from the station with two ladies when it collided with the tram car. All the glass was broken and one lady was rather badly cut. The driver got on the taxi to try to make it go. But it would not move. He then bent down and got a revolver from somewhere near his seat and blew his brains out. The shock to the ladies was worse than the accident. No one else bothered about it. A very short notice was in the evening paper and we shall hear no more of it. Lives are not valued so much here.

Monday 8th March.

I went to Hannover by order of the police to get a passport from the American consul. It was a real treat to get out of the town for a few hours. I saw Mr. Plunkett who is still at home as he was too ill to go to Ruhleben. He seems very delicate.

I was very much surprised to see the floods between here and Hannover. There were miles and miles of meadow and field under water. A farmer (at present a soldier of course) who was travelling into Hannover told us that they had to pump the water out of the cow and horse stalls each morning. But if we had no frost it would do no harm. Last February they were flooded three times and it did not kill the wheat because there was no frost. This farmer told us that the next call up of men would empty his district. Practically all who were able to go had offered themselves free willing.

Food is very dear. Potatoes are seven shillings a hundredweight. And bread is ten pence for five pounds and you can only buy a certain quantity.

Tuesday & Wednesday 9th & 10th March.

We hear of great loses to the English, both in France and the Dardanelles, and many French and English have been taken prisoners. We also hear of a German undersea boat being lost,U12, sank by an English, or French boat. But it seems the Germans sank five ships on Monday . Today they are able to give their names but I fancy they are trading vessels.

We are informed today that the weight of bread is to be reduced to six ounces (200 grams) for all over six-years-old and for those less than six-years-old only three ounces (100 grams) only is allowed per day. We are informed that the potatoes are to be weighed out after this week.

I went to the bank today for my usual amount for the month, twenty pounds, and was informed that they dare not give me more than five pounds and I must make it last as long as I can.

Had a letter from Arthur today and he still has hope of coming out. I have none. All I speak to are of the same opinion.

Thursday 11th March.

The collection of gold is announced today and I hear that we still have one million pounds worth of gold in circulation.

Our school has a holiday so we do not go to give out the milk.

Each school that brings one hundred and fifty pounds worth of gold to the collection gets a holiday. So all the children visit their relations and get the gold from them and they in turn receive the value in paper money. This school through its various scholars raised one hundred and seventy pounds in gold and so had a free day.

All householders have received a ticket from the police and must say how many potatoes they have in store. Many men have been sent into Belgium to work the fields there and plant ready for next year.

Friday 12th March.

The hotel is full up with officers and their wives. The men have to go to the front next week and their wives have come to stay the last few days with them. It's very sad. I met a lady today, Frau von Ludwich, and her husband has been sent for. He is fifty-three-years-old. He was an officer for thirteen years and has been away from the army for twenty years. He goes to take the place of officers who have been called to the front. In the last battle in the Champagne the losses were very great on the French and English side, as well as the German, and also in the Carpathians.

Hermenia's brother is there and he has written home that two weeks ago a regiment went into battle and only twenty-eight returned. I asked how many a company was. They say that in war time the number of men and officers is five hundred and twenty-five. That seems a dreadful loss to me.

No news of the Dardanelles but it is reported that Greece, Italy and Romania are German friendly.

Saturday 13th March.

Today they say that it is not true that C.H. Beresford, the British Admiral, stated, 'I would hang all German sailors as pirates' the next time he took any as prisoners. I had said at the time it was published that I did not believe it. The Germans said they did. I had no excuse good enough for the British sailor as he is a noted cruel man. However it was my time to crow for the German government said it was untrue.

Six hundred soldiers go from here today and six hundred more will leave one day next week. Von Hindenburg has sent word from Russia that he must have another hundred thousand men in fourteen days. He had one hundred thousand men in January (sent in three days notice) so the men must be falling there. They go away quite bravely but openly say they would rather be cold in Russia than face the French guns. They never cease and they are very good shots.

I talked today with the daughter of Herr Grebe. She has only been married one year and her husband is seven months in the field. She tells me that she must send him each week a large packet of food which costs her at least ten shillings. She has two soldiers quartering in her home. She must give them coffee and butter in the morning (they get their bread from the government) and a buttered sandwich for lunch. They have dinner in the barracks. Then in the evening she cooks them a hot soup or gives them some sort of supper. They have a good bed and fire and she gets for each man one penny per day from the government.

Each person who pays five shillings per week rent must put up one soldier, seven shillings per week rent must put up two soldiers and ten shillings per week rent must put up three soldiers.

After that it depends on the amount of rooms you have. In this hotel the proprietor must put up, for one penny per day, sixteen men. He has turned a large restaurant into a little barracks and he also takes in soldiers who are impossible to have. These householders pay another nine pence a man to the hotel keeper for each week they cannot put them up. It makes for a deal of expense and work but nobody grumbles.

My passport came from the American Consul.

Sunday 14th March.

We were very busy yesterday trying to buy a little bread. But it is an impossibility to get one pennyworth without a card from the police. The bread we have is too awful for words and has made Belle and me ill. So we are running after 'Graham Brot'. This is like our Hovis bread and is only sold to invalids. I told Belle that she must go to the police for a card as she looks just like an invalid. She is so thin. I am just as fat. I believe that if I lived on air for a month I should still be fat.

Arthur writes me that he has gone much thinner. I envy him.

Monday 15th March.

William Steinoff came to see me. He is busy this week getting all the potatoes and corn to the government. Each person can only keep enough to seed next year and food for one month. After that the farmers themselves must buy corn for food from the government.

Tuesday 16th March.

News today of the sinking of four English merchant ships but only a few lives were lost. The same torpedo boat has sunk them that sunk the Cressy etc. but we hear nothing of the Dardanelles. The Germans acknowledge a repulse by the English and say they were driven back a short way on March 9th. They hope to get all back in a few days.

Wednesday 17th March.

St. Patrick's Day and is such a nice day here. It is quite like spring.

We have no war news, only the usual (a small advance in France) but we hear of a lot of men are going before Warsaw and taking the larger guns which nothing can withstand. Perhaps we shall soon hear of the fall of Warsaw.

There are a lot of new regulations this week for the outlander and it gives me a deal of anxiety.

I wrote to Ettie and dad these last few days. I do hope they get them.

Thursday 18th March.

We hear the English have sunk the German boat Dresden and it gives great sorrow. I hope no lives are lost.

I haven't heard from Arthur for ten days. I hope he is well.

Friday 19th March.

Bad news today. One French warship and one English warship have been sunk off the Dardanelles. It is reported that the English and French have been sent back with great losses.

The Russians are again in East Prussia. We did not hear when they came in but it is a report from Hindenburg. It seems as if this war will last a long time.

Notices have been posted this week that after this week that motor driven carriages cannot be used. All petrol and oil and spirits in your possession must be sent to the government so no taxis after next week. There have been very few for some time – drivers and oil being very scarce. Men keep leaving here suddenly.

The bread is scarcer this week and you can hardly buy it at all. The white bread is a little better. They say it is because we get more wheat from the farmers than rye or barley.

Saturday & Sunday 20th – 21st March.

I was ill.

Monday 22nd March.

We read that the Socialists are grumbling in the parliament. It does not avail them anything.

Joseph Koch goes tomorrow to his regiment. He only passed his solicitors exam last Thursday. I congratulated him on his success, to which he replied: 'Yes, if I live to get any good out of it'.

I feel very sorry for his people. I hoped they could keep one son out of four at home. He is the last and he goes tomorrow.

Tuesday 23rd March.

We hear today of the fall of Przemysl and that the Russians have been driven out of Memel. So once more the German land is clear of Russians. In taking Przemysl from the Austrians the Russians got over forty thousand prisoners. They had no more food I hear.

Stoffregan and Steinoff came to see me today and both are in want of the orchard and the garden. I wish the house was let and settled.

Wednesday 24th March.

No war news, only a lot of accounts of the fall of Przemysl. It is reported that two hundred people per day for the last two weeks have died of hunger. The Austrians burned all of value before giving in and the report here is that the Russians have gained very little.

I was ill and had to go to the doctor but now feel a little better.

Received a postcard from Arthur, the first in eighteen days, saying he was well and I must send him his summer clothes.

Sunday 28th March.

It is Palm Sunday and a great day here. The Protestants have confirmation and the streets are full of visitors to the ceremony for all members of the family are invited. One family gave the dinner at half-past-four and eighteen people sat down.

The girls are all in black with black gloves and wear myrtle wreaths. The boys are all in navy blue, or black, suits with black gloves and ties with a spray of myrtle in their coats. It is such a business and all friends send congratulations, flowers, and a present. Watches and umbrellas are much in demand.

Milk is announced as scarcer and dearer and the oil coke has run out. Belle and I went into four shops this morning to buy French toilet soap and people were scarcely civil to us.

No news from the Dardanelles or Flanders, but a small notice to say the usual advance in Russia and France. People are getting tired of reading it. Belle and I were reading the usual last week and a gentleman said: 'I am tired of seeing the same old news. It's always the same'.

So it does not seem as if the public believe all of it.

We read from a neutral paper that the English have got the inner six forts of the Dardanelles and that they expect them to fall about Easter. Here we read nothing of it.

Many more soldiers are called up again this week. Six thousand go from Hannover province next week to the front. That is eighteen thousand men since Christmas from this province alone. In Hildesheim today we have eleven thousand men in uniform.

Monday & Tuesday 29th & 30th March.

No war news just a short notice to the effect – 'We have made small advances west and east'. We have had nothing else for some days – only the fall of Przemysl.

I went for the last time to give out milk to the poor children. The school closes tomorrow for sixteen days, so no more milk this term. Carole Osthaus, the relation I go with to the school, asked the manager of the place if it would commence again in the autumn. He said: 'If Germany wins certainly but if we lose no one can tell about the milk'.

I was surprised for it is the first time that a doubt of them winning has ever been expressed publicly. One can see that they are uneasy. It was never doubted that all would be over in four months at the latest.

Having no war news they are again attacking the English. All hotels which had an English name have changed them to a Prussian one. The notices are very frequent in the shops – 'God punish the English'. They never seem to think it is a reflection on their religion or what they prize far more – their 'culture'.

We had a very amusing incident here last week and I roared laughing. Belle got angry and said so. We went into a shop where I have spent a deal of money at times and, of course, they know that Arthur is a prisoner. I am pretty quick at noticing and at once saw the notice 'God punish etc.' hung in a prominent place. While the assistant was serving me the proprietor came in and took down the notice. He put it under the counter in a great hurry. I told Belle of it and laughed a great deal. She said what she thought and remarked that when they (the shop workers) say 'good morning' that she does not even say it back to such unworthy people. She is German so it did not matter. But I am English.

I asked the head waiter to buy me a sign as I wanted it for some German friends in England. But he did not get me one.

Wednesday 31st March.

No war news. We have a paper a month old from America and what a treat.

Two waiters went in six hours notice to the army. One is the head waiter and he is the only one who knows a word of English. I am now alone in my glory!

Thursday & Friday 1st & 2nd April 1915.

Good Friday is a lovely spring day and we have spent a lot of time in church. This war has made the Catholics very devout and all services are full. When you think there are eight large churches in Hildesheim it means many people in church. The Protestants are not nearly so devout. The services are very beautiful and I never saw such a lovely altar of repose as the one at the Dom. In the evening we had a fine sermon by a Franciscan monk. He brought the lesson of the war in, said how we were ahead the first few weeks, and now we must wait God's time.

Saturday & Sunday 3rd & 4th April.

Today is Easter Sunday and still no news of the war. The papers are full of China and Japan. I wonder if it will come to anything.

The papers keep telling us little memories of Bismarck but I think it is to keep our minds on the war. April the 1st was the hundredth birthday of Bismarck and every

German town celebrated it. The town was decorated in the morning and everyone wore a button. It is a general holiday. In the evening there was a speech and a few national songs in the Town Hall square. Then the people walked in procession to the Bismarck statue which is twenty minutes away. The statue was decorated and there were more songs and fireworks. An English lady who had never seen a German crowd before was astonished at the quietness and orderliness of the thing. No loud laughing and screaming like there would have been in England. At nine o'clock at night there was nothing but the greatest reverence and respect.

This acknowledges that we in England can learn a lot from the German conduct.

We had a fine sermon today, quite out of the ordinary. The Pastor had received a letter from a parishioner, not by any means noted for his piety when here, and he read us a portion of it and took his sermon from the same. It was a sad letter and very likely the same man was now shot. He said that if he was alive he would think of his church this Easter Sunday morning but his organ would be a cannon, his hymns the bombs, and the shrapnel the prayers for his comrades shot before his eyes. The Pastor said his letter was written on Tuesday and perhaps by Wednesday he was dead. His religion was his only comfort.

So much that one hears these days is too sad to live through.

Monday 5th April.

There is a notice in the paper today that the government has issued orders that no extra telegrams will be issued during the Easter holidays. It sounds as if there have been some reverses at the front. I am only anxious over the Dardanelles but not a word is to be heard. England has said they cannot be taken before Easter and I am hoping for some news soon.

I had dinner with Belle yesterday and we drank Arthur's health in his own champagne. I had a few bottles sent from the house and on special occasions we toast him in Ruhleben and drink his champagne or wine. Fine is it not? I only wish I could send him a few bottles.

Tuesday & Wednesday 6th & 7th April.

It is lovely spring weather and the trees seem to have become covered in green in just a day or so.

I went to the doctor yesterday. I have been going for two weeks or more and he told me that he did not think I should have my husband for a long time yet.

Thursday 8th April.

It is reported today that **U29** has been lost. It has been missing since the 27th March and they hoped to hear daily from her. Now they think she has been sunk by the English whilst she was helping passengers to leave a sinking ship. I reminded our waiter that about the 28th March there was a report in the Hildesheim paper that - 'The British Admiralty has announced the sinking of an undersea boat by an English ship but they could not see her number. After the shooting it sank and never reappeared'. This announcement was under the heading of 'More British lies' and I remember it well. They will not have it so here. They say she has either struck a mine or the English have sunk her whilst rescuing passengers from a sinking ship. What ship we are not told.

Friday 9th April.

We read today of an uprising of the people of Italy and of them being against Germany. The papers are full of it and apparently Italy is a dreadful nation. I never knew it.

Saturday 10th April.

A funny thing happened yesterday. I quite forgot to go to the police and chased around at half-past-three. I have to go before one o'clock. I had wild visions of being escorted by a couple of policemen which is not an unlikely thing. You can bet that I was not five minutes in getting there. I made great apologies and they graciously forgave me. They told me that I must not do it again or I become a penalty.

Got a letter from Arthur and he seems to be very well and comfortable and says that they had a fine concert on Good Friday. There were over forty fine performers and they presented the bandmaster with a new conducting stick. The presentation was made by a Mr. Butterworth of Manchester. Arthur has written before of there being several good musical artists imprisoned and also several painters. There is a small chapel now built and they have mass every fourteen days. I wonder if it is like Dresden. At the commencement of the war Mass was stopped at the English church in Dresden but later reopened. Police were present at each service to be sure that no prayers were offered up for England. I should imagine that they would take the same precautions in Ruhleben.

Sunday 11th April.

No news from the front. China and Japan are quiet again and no sign of war.

I had a letter from Alice Graeinghoff yesterday. She writes to me that there are many German prisoners at Handforth and that the rescued men of the Blücher are there. Lena went to see them one day and met a man from Königswinter and he was able to speak to her. She wrote to his father for him to say he was very comfortable.

Monday 12th April.

Our Willie's birthday. It's a lovely day here. The war news is the usual – a small advance in the east and west.

I sent Arthur a parcel and I have advertised the house again and hope I can let it.

Miss Broches leaves for Switzerland and says she will write to my people for me from there.

Many more Landstorm are called up today. All are men of forty or so and I do feel sorry for them. This morning I heard many feet going past the hotel at half-past-three and they were soldiers going to the barracks. They were to go on a sixty kilometre (forty English miles) march starting off at four o'clock and to arrive back at half-past-one. They are fitted up just as if for the front. I saw them come in at half-past-one passing the hotel. Many were limping and all looked dead tired. These men go away in ten days and are mostly for Russia.

We hear today in the German papers that the English have been sent back by the Turks at the Dardanelles and all is quiet there.

Tuesday 13th April.

There is the usual list of small fishing boats sunk by torpedo but that is all. There is an announcement to the effect of having heard that the English people have put the rescued men from the U boats in prison and treated them as pirates. The Germans have taken four English officers for each one of the Germans and are treating them just the same. Four for one - that is the German justice - not one for one. I think it is very dishonourable. I cannot think that the English people, who are renowned for their fairness, can punish men who are only doing what they are told.

There are a lot more men called up today and these are not free willing. One never hears them singing as they march through the streets. The free willing were much more lusty.

There is another attempt to revive the English hate. I firmly believe that the hatred is based on the fact of there being no conscription in England. The first thing a German man says to you is: 'After this war Englishmen must be like us – under conscription'.

That is a great pleasure to him. I remarked that I did not think so and the reply was: 'This will make them'.

I said that England would have a revolution first. Oh, I would not wish that misery for England.

Wednesday 14th April.

Went to Woltershausen for half a day to see about the garden but I can get no workers. Steinoff tells me there are no more men to go away from our village. All are gone who are between nineteen years and forty-five and that it is the same in the neighbouring villages. He also tells me that Hans, our old horse, has gone to the front and also that the dog Uncle George took with him, Lord, has died. So with the horse and dog the last of our pets are gone.

Thursday 15th April.

I saw a lot of men going to Berlin today. It was such a sad sight. They had been called up to the Commando here and all the tallest men were sent away to Berlin to take their place in the Guards regiment. That regiment has suffered very severely in France. There was a procession of over three hundred men and they had been called up for fifty miles around here and all were men from thirty to forty-five. They walked along with their cardboard boxes and never looked up. It was very easy to place them in their various grades of life – the merchant, teacher, priest, parson, bank clerk, musician and worker. I cried as I saw them and so did many more women.

I went to the Doctor's and when I got there a woman, who was watching the procession from the windows in the Doctor's rooms, asked me if my husband was amongst them for she could see that I had been crying. I said no – my husband was already away.

She said: 'So is mine. But I am past crying. Many of the wives of these poor men expect them home tonight, but they will get a telegram from Berlin instead'.

She went on to say: 'This war has killed as many women as men. I know a few who have died when they knew their husbands were killed or injured. The doctor has told me it's no use me coming again to him until the war is ended, for it is anxiety that is killing me'.

And she looked it.

When I got back to the hotel I found that three of the waiters had been sent for and now we only had one for the week. He took the place of the head waiter. It's awful for the proprietor as the hotel is quite full of officers and is very much understaffed. Women are doing a lot of men's work but they do not act as waiters here.

There is a collection from house to house of old India rubber this week. They ask for all kinds of old gum shoes, mackintoshes, old hot water bottles, anything made of rubber and no matter how small. The woollen and metal collections were a great success.

Friday 16th April.

Three hundred men leave here today for Russia.

I feel so sorry for the chambermaid as she is so upset for her brother-in-law. He goes to the front today for the fourth time. He has been wounded three times and says he does not care if the next bullet or bomb finishes him. He suffered so much with his wound last time that he dreads going away. It seems as if they are getting tired of it. All long for peace.

Saturday 17th April.

We hear that an airship has been over Kent and that it has done a deal of damage. We do not have many details. They seem uneasy over Italy and Greece. There is no news of the Dardanelles or Prussia.

Had a postcard from Arthur saying he wished me to go away to a baths for a change. Perhaps I will after I have finished with the doctor.

Belle and I have been buying things to send to a friend at the front in Russia. When we were buying a lady in the shop said to me: 'Is your son at the front?'

Belle and I laughed about it but I thought: 'Well, I must look old'.

If I looked as old as I felt she would have asked me if it was my grandson who was at the front.

Everything is dear. Butter is one-shilling-and-nine-pence per pound, bread (rye) two pence per pound, white bread four-and-half pence per pound and we can only get a quarter pound per day or six ounces of brown (rye) – more than that you cannot buy. The system of bread tickets is working very well and you can get no more. I know of families who have to eat potatoes every night. All sausage is six pence per pound dearer and meat is also very dear. It's a good thing that summer is coming. I wonder how long it will last.

I was speaking to a woman today whose husband was at home from France on a week's leave. He said that some of the neutral countries should, in mercy, have arbitration to stop the war for it was only murder. No one was making headway and there were murders everyday. I also heard that a man who had returned to the front said he got a shock when he got back and that he greatly feared a pestilence next summer in the ranks.

The men who are going now are not young and they have seen more than the first lot. They are not so keen. Besides they have wives and children to leave behind.

Sunday & Monday 18th & 19th April.

There is news of the English being sent back at the Dardanelles and of the French attacking the Germans. But they made no progress and that the loss of life was great.

It is perfect spring weather and much too warm to wear a coat. Lots of people are in full summer outfits.

Arthur wrote me on Saturday and wants Belle and I to get away for a month to a bath or into the mountains. But I have not yet finished with the doctor.

Tuesday 20th April.

We read today that the English government is sending four pounds of flour per person per week to their prisoners here. That's a godsend for the bread here is dreadful. Arthur often gets a parcel from his English friends of tobacco and cigars and he always writes bright letters. I am now glad he is where he is. If he was free he would have been at the front by now.

The last few lots to go were all over forty-years-old and so many of them had bad eyesight and weak hearts. They have to be very ill when they are passed over now.

Herr Grebe told me of a friend of his who was sent to the front after being shot in the lungs. He has spit blood ever since and was spitting it when he went away.

The doctor said: 'The good weather is coming and you will pick up'

We are getting dark bread now at two pence per pound and white bread at four-and-a-half pence per pound. I wonder if they are paying nine pence for a two pound loaf in England.

Herr Stoffregan went to a sale of a farm in Adenstedt and the dried beans for cattle fetched thirty-six shillings per hundredweight. The usual price is fourteen shillings. Everything is dearer now and it is impossible to buy bread without a card from the magistrate and your allowance is only one third of a pound per day. The difference must be made up of soup or potatoes.

Everywhere there is a shortage of men. If you go in a shop it is all young men, or women, who serve you. They never complain. Such unity surprises me. With just one half to put up with the English man would grumble for hours. There is always the firm belief of the winning and always the same talk. England is always to blame for all this war and bloodshed.

Wednesday & Thursday 21ˢᵗ & 22ⁿᵈ April.

I paid a visit yesterday to Dean Heiser and we of course talked about the war. He is confident of Germany winning and he does not think the war will last long. The Dardanelles are impossible to take he says and the English are as usual too stupid to know that they are wasting lives and ammunition on a false hope. He has a firm belief in England's ignorance of warfare and feels sorry for her soldiers under such fools of officers and ministers.

Friday & Saturday 23ʳᵈ & 24ᵗʰ April.

We hear today of a great battle by Ypres in Flanders. A great victory for Germany and there are many thousands of French and English prisoners and dead. Also they have captured thirty large English cannons. The Germans have made a great forward march. It does not state that they have yet got Ypres.

Sunday 25ᵗʰ April.

There is a good account in the papers of many bank officials being let out of Ruhleben. It was very amusing to read of their journey from Berlin to Hamburg. The person who wrote the account for the papers had a full share of hate for the English. He complained bitterly of the Germans having to stand up on a crowded train while Englishmen sat at their ease in first class carriages and in the dining car. You could hear the pop of champagne corks. It was dreadful. There were the poor Germans full of troubles and thinking of their people on the battlefield and too sad to smile. And there were the cheeky English, in an enemy's land, feeding and drinking. So said the correspondent!

Monday 26th April.

The papers report a great progress in Flanders. Over three thousand five hundred prisoners and many killed. There is no report of any losses.

Belle told me that she made a visit to the Bishop and was surprised to hear him say that, with the exception of one here and one there, that the English were very unsatisfactory as a nation and that the politics were very rotten in that land. In fact there is nothing good about the general crowd if only one or two stand out alone. This is from an educated man who has never been to England. It is astonishing that they give their opinions.

I heard from Arthur and cannot send him anymore tobacco or cigars.

Wednesday 28th April.

The Germans are making a great way in Flanders but it is not announced that Ypres is in their hands.

I had a visit from Miss Marhgraf today and she had an American friend with her, a Californian, and she has had a <u>bad</u> time here.

Today we had two flying machines over the town. This was great excitement for one was supposed to be an enemy ship. The Germans all have the iron cross painted on them but this one was plain and did not drop the usual flag over the town. These things are common here and we often see a Zeppelin labelled 'For London'. It is very weird to hear them fly over a town at night. You are in your bed and you hear the great motors whizzing and wonder if it is an enemy and if a bomb can fall. It is not pleasant. At night they fly so low and you can hear them plainly. Then another night many autos will race through the town at great speed and you wonder if Paris has fallen or what on earth is the matter. It is a time of great excitement and I shall be thankful when it is all over. The wonder is that so many people can live through it for so many are ill.

Thursday 29th April.

Still great progress is reported by Ypres and it makes one hope that the end is not far off.

I saw a lot of soldiers selling their bicycles today. I suppose it's their last week here. There were so many and they were standing outside the shop - each with his bike.

Hermenia tells me that all the potatoes are gone from Woltershausen and at a good price. Fancy - pigs are fifty-eight shillings a cut alive. That is a price.

Saturday 1st May 1915.

The people are very angry with America deciding to supply England with ammunition and say that she does not think of lives – just dollars.

Flying machines go over here every day and are almost as common as the birds in the air.

I went today to see a man just out of Ruhleben. He has got leave for two months because he is ill and he gave me a lot of interesting news. He says it will be all right in summer but in the winter it was so cold. Arthur eats in the canteen and can draw the amount of ten shillings a week from his money. It's not so bad if you have cash to buy what you fancy though there is not too great a choice. It's awful if you have no money at all. He had a model of the place and had written some poetry on it. He has also made some funny sketches and we did laugh over them. He thinks the war will not last two months longer as it is being felt in all places of business and is easily seen.

Steinoff and Stoffregan came to see me and I do not know what to do about the garden for no labour can be got.

Sunday 2nd May.

No further news of the big battle in Flanders but we hear of the terrible Canadian losses. Even here they speak of their bravery. And that is something.

I asked today how it was that the soldiers did not sing any more. I was told that many people who had lost relatives in the war had asked the military not to allow it in the streets. They could not bear to hear it after their losses of sons and husbands.

Monday 3rd May.

There is great rejoicing today. The Russians have been driven out of the Carpathians and the Germans and

Austrians claim a great victory. Over a hundred thousand guns, sixty eight thousand men and four hundred officers, prisoners and the war material would fill a newspaper column with all kinds of food and goods and ammunition. The flags are flying and for the first time. The Turkish and German and Austrian are flying together so I suppose that the Turks have helped a great deal.

No news of the Dardanelles but a very strange article about the Kaiser's brother, Prince Henri of Prussia, is in the papers. They say he is Admiral of the Fleet but he refuses to have anything to do with this war and people are asking questions.

I wrote a long letter to Arthur today and had coffee with Herr Mummers and his cousin on the Steinberg. It was a perfect day and the view was lovely. It was the last walk Arthur, Belle and I took the evening before he went away.

On our return we read extra telegrams saying a further increase of prisoners and another victory in Russia and it gives thirty thousand prisoners and a lot more ammunition and guns etc.

Herr Mummer's cousin told me that everything in the food lines was just double the price with the exception of coffee and sugar. Coffee is a little dearer but sugar is at the old price yet. Green vegetables are an awful price and a cabbage costs eighty-two pfennigs or ten pence halfpenny.

Wednesday 5th May.

Today we read that the victory report last night was false. Someone has forged the name of '**WOLF**'. This is the only telegram we can rely on (it is supposed to be better than Reuters) and it said that the flags must all be put away.

A great many soldiers go away today. Half go to Russia and half go to France. Now there is a great deal of difference between the men and those before Christmas. These men are so sad. I heard one man remark: 'This war is lasting too long'.

It is telling on the businesses and you scarcely see anyone in the banks.

Thursday 6th May.

Had a postcard from Arthur today and he says he is trying to get an allowance to visit for two weeks. I hope that he gets it if only to put things in order here.

For a few weeks now we have had soldiers guarding the flour mill here. We have a very large flour mill called 'The Bishop's Mill' as it formerly belonged to the Prince Bishop of Hildesheim. Now it belongs to the town though still bearing the name of the Bishop. All during the war it has been as usual but since April it has been guarded by soldiers doing sentry duty.

There is great uneasiness over Italy. <u>Of course,</u> England is at the bottom of it.

We had great trouble yesterday. A cousin of Arthur and Belle was buried. He was only fifteen-years-old and we are afraid he has committed suicide. He was such a bright noble looking boy and so tall. We met him last Thursday by the river and this Thursday he is buried. We can get to know nothing of his death and suicides are not put in the paper here. We shall hear in time from the family.

The schools have a holiday to celebrate the Russians being sent out of the Carpathians.

Friday 7th May.

There is an announcement of many English prisoners being taken in Flanders and great unrest over Italy. There is also an announcement that all Germans must clear out of Italy and that all Italians are being called up. They will not find Germany unprepared as they have expected Italy to be deceitful.

Saturday 8th May.

We hear today with great grief of the sinking of the **Lusitania**. It is a terrible thing. Here, of course, it is looked on as a great and skilful piece of work and never a pitiful word for the lives lost. The Germans say that the boat was armed and that they are quite within their rights. They talk of it as a great deed done.

Sunday 9th May.

There are special telegrams issued today about the way the news was received in America and of the disturbance there. It appears that the German Ambassador was very badly handled. Well, so were people here in the excitement of the war but no one remembers that now.

They say that King George has sent a telegram of congratulations to the Dardanelles and they say that the English are easily pleased with a victory. It has only been the gaining of about two miles of land.

George von Brounswigh, the young cousin who died, had suddenly gone out of his mind with a rush of blood to the head. He travelled from here to Magdeburg and bought a wreath. He put it on his father's grave and then shot himself. He was alive and losing blood when found and he came to his senses. They sent for his mother but he was dead when she got there. I have such sorrow for her for he was a fine boy and only fifteen-years-old. He inherited a large estate two years ago from an uncle and now there is no one to take it of that name. It is a great pity.

I have sent for Father Gatsemire to call on me to get some Masses said for mother and grandmother and I hope that he comes today. It was mother's anniversary last week.

I saw crowds of children on Saturday outside the soldier's barracks trying to buy bread from them. The soldiers get so much per week and it is very good bread. With these bread tickets people with a family do not get enough. Children eat more than six ounces per day so they try to buy from the soldiers. It was so funny to see the soldiers plaguing them.

Monday 10th May.

There is a lot in the paper about the sinking of the **Lusitania**. Germany has warned America that if they let any more ships go to England after their refusal to stop supplying ammunition that they, the Germans, should sink all ships. America and England only laughed so now they see that the Germans are as good as their word. They maintain here that the Lusitania was fitted up as a battleship and had five big guns and a quantity of ammunition. They say that they were within their rights to sink her and seem surprised that there should be any fuss over it. Some of the more feeling people express sorrow that it has been done. Still it is owing to England that it has been done at all.

It is a blessing that Italy at present is receiving a little hatred and England is a little forgotten. It's dreadful to hear the sermons about the falseness of Italy and what should be done to the Italians here. I should hate any Englishman who so far forgot himself as to express the hatred you hear of here in Germany.

All the papers ridicule the fact that anyone makes any progress only the Germans. Yet if the others are losing at all places why are they, the Italians, going to join the losing side?

Of course there is no freedom of the press here. Everything seems to be controlled. Just fancy this – a youth here, seventeen-years-old and an only son of a lawyer wanted to go free willing into the army. His father told him that after he had done his examinations and finished his studies he could go, very likely this autumn, and then he would have lost no time with his studies. The authorities got to know about this at the school and one day last week the father received a letter. It told him that if he did not let his son go at once then he would not be allowed to sit the exam in the autumn.

People tell of one another here. If you do or say anything that shows that anything else comes before the Fatherland then the police always get to know. I often wondered why people whispered when they mentioned some things. To an English person this is dreadful.

Gosbert von Ludwich, seventeen-years-old and a very delicate looking boy, had offered himself, free willing, just before Easter. He went to the officers' school at once because he intends to make the army his profession and after a few weeks training he goes this week to Warsaw as an officer. His training has been severe and I cannot think that he is quite ready yet. His mother did not expect it so soon and she is upset.

Tuesday 11th May.

There is great excitement over Italy. They think she will go into war. The Kaiser has written himself and there is yet a faint hope of peace.

Belle tells me that she reads from a neutral report that England has landed troops at the Dardanelles and already has shooting graves dug. This has never been in our papers and I wonder if they will get the Dardanelles. It also states that America has sent a demand to know what of this disaster with the **Lusitania**. She refuses to hear anything only the words of the commander of the torpedo boat who sank her. They will have no one else report.

There is an account of the estate of Baron Reuter being confiscated. This is the Reuter who sends the telegrams for England from all over the world. He is a German but has become naturalised.

They told me at the bank one day that if a German died and left anyone in enemy land money or goods that these would be confiscated. As an Englander I should get nothing if Arthur died and it would all go to the crown. <u>Arthur had better keep well</u>.

Wednesday 12th May.

No war news of any note only great unrest over Italy and a certain insult if we go into a shop to buy anything Italian. The people's nerves are all on edge. They are certain of winning if they can keep Italy out. Even then they will win but the war will last longer.

Thursday 13th May.

It is Ascension Thursday so a general Sunday and all people are fine. The shops are open for one hour only. It is lovely weather and every promise of a good year.

It is the usual war news. The English sent back from the Dardanelles and the Germans making headway in France.

Friday 14th May.

News of a warship being sunk by the Turks and Germans at the Dardanelles, the **Goliath,** and they report five hundred men drowned.

Great excitement is reported in England about a visit of a Zeppelin over Southend. They say that the English attacked the Germans and that the police want all the naturalised Germans to be put in prison (like Arthur) for their own good. The temper of the people is so very bitter. I hope the Englishman will have more sense than to get the name for himself that the German has. I hope that he will leave hatred to this country alone. For it is beneath an Englishman's character.

Our coachman (from the hotel) went to the military today, poor fellow. He is not at all strong and suffers from consumption but he had to go. He coughs dreadfully and spits up blood also. I suppose that is why he has been left to the last. There are not many left from twenty to forty-five-years-old.

Saturday 15th May.

Went to the bank today and told the banker that I thought of going to the Harz Mountains. He told me to stay where I was for the people in Germany were very angry at the way the Germans were being treated in England. He remarked that the accounts in the papers were dreadful. He said if I was in a place that I was not known that it might go very bad with me.

I shall decide to stay here as this is much safer.

Food is very dear, butter is one shilling and ten pence a pound and lard is one shilling and eight pence (they use it here on bread a great deal) and the cheapest meat is one shilling and six pence a pound. Green vegetables are at a discount. Old potatoes are at one and a half pence a pound and you can only have so many. Oil and benzene are a dreadful price and you are limited to a pint a week.

There are long notices out warning the people to be careful, and especially in the kitchen. The winter is to be dreaded if the war continues. Dried foods like beans (haricot) and peas are an awful price. They are six pence and eight pence a pound. Rice is not to be got, and also sago. Cocoa and chocolate are very scarce and English people are not allowed to buy them. It is the same with tobacco and cigars.

Sunday 16th May.

They report a sharp note from America, but do not give us the contents.

I saw Frau Ernst today, the sister-in-law of Steffen, and she tells me that they have not heard from her brother for four weeks and are uneasy. He was in Flanders and he had a sudden order for Russia but did not know what part. He then wrote them he was in Russia, but again he did not know what part. The soldiers were three-and-a- half days in the train and then had an eighty kilometre march over dreadful land. They were now at the front, but still knowing not where. Frau Ernst feels very uneasy for he used to write regularly.

Monday 17th May.

Serious news today for it seems likely that Italy will go to war and everyone is in mourning. You have to turn around to see anyone in colour.

Sunday 23rd May.

I feel a little better, not much, and am still on a diet of one quart of buttermilk per day with nothing else to eat. I have only lost four pounds in a week. It's rotten to feel ill in a hotel.

Today the place is full of soldiers and their friends as they have two days holiday. Here Sunday and Monday are the same two Sundays together and everyone goes to Mass and keep Monday as little Sunday. It's sad to see the soldiers with their relatives. One young soldier has passed here with his mother on his arm and she is such a feeble old lady. There are crowds of soldiers with their wives and children. The father is ready for the field in his grey uniform (they only stay here a few days after they get their grey clothes) and often he is carrying one little thing and the mother another with one or two more holding on to their clothes. The parents are looking anything but bright. It is a sight on a Sunday night to go to the station and see the people leaving their soldier sons and husbands here. It is too sad for words.

They are down in the mouth over Italy and say that they will soon make that dirty place clean and will never forgive her for her falseness.

No war news of any importance and the papers are full of Italy and a few untruths. One of the untruths is that the English people have offered the Pope ten thousand pounds a year to go and live in England. <u>That</u> did make me laugh. We do not know what this is about. Perhaps the English Cabinet, in time, will let us know.

Monday 24th May.

Nothing to report except Italy. Already we read how her papers lie and no one gets the truth - only we in Germany. There is one report of the whole regiment (Italian) being against this war and have all run away to Switzerland. I said that I admired them and that I also would run away before I would be made to fight in a cause I thought wrong. I also said that every man in the field ought to be free willing.

Tuesday 25th May.

Been to Woltershausen today and things seem bad in the food line. Steinoff gave me a list of the increase in prices he is paying – it's really dreadful.

Maize for hens is now twenty-seven shillings per hundredweight - before it was seven shillings. Beans for cows & pigs are now thirty-six shillings per hundredweight - before they were eleven shillings per hundredweight. Rice for chickens is now seven pence per pound - before it was two pence per pound. And so on.

Pigs, he tells me, are fetching ninety-five to a hundred shillings per hundredweight alive and little pigs, six-weeks-old, twenty-six shillings each. Before the war they were fourteen shillings and forty shillings per hundredweight and that was good for live pigs.

I am not much stronger and the doctor says I had better get some stronger air as I lost six-and-a-half pounds in a week. I am glad of that but I feel so weakly.

We hear tonight that the Russians have had great losses by Przemysl. Twenty-three thousand prisoners and a lot of guns were taken. They never seem to know when they are getting surrounded though we can see it on the map for days before.

Wednesday & Thursday 26th & 27th May.

There is news of an English ship, the **Majestic**, being lost and news of the Italians being in a fight in the mountains. The Austrians won of course. The Italians are such cowards. As soon as they heard the big guns they ran away.

Saturday 29th May.

Hear of the English being sent back at the Dardanelles and the loss of another ship. The Germans complain that the English will not come out to fight and her ships are all in harbour.

Today a canary flew into my room. He is so tame. I shall keep him.

Sunday 30th May.

Got a letter from our Willie today and it is over two months since anyone wrote me a line. They must write more often.

Thursday 3rd June.

Corpus Christie and a fine feast day here. We hear of the capture of Przemysl and the Russians have lost heavily. The Germans have retaken the place but it is Austrian of course. The Russians took it about three weeks ago. They (the Russians) do not seem to know what they are doing.

Today it is announced that we must prepare for next winter and that the women must get their wool at once from the Rathaus (town hall) and commence knitting for the winter. Carole Osthaus has got some. All the socks that were used last winter have had the feet worn away so all the legs are washed and unwoven. This year we are short of wool so the legs of the socks are being knitted out of thick cotton and the feet are knitted out of the wool taken from last years socks. They are very practical here. I am sure their war is costing them less than any other country that is in the field. Everyone works so very well together and the organisation is marvellous. If it were only so in the other countries then much suffering would be saved.

Friday - Sunday 4th - 6th June.

A French flyer has been over the Crown Prince's quarters and dropped bombs but there is not much damage. A German flyer has been over Harwich and set many places on fire.

Yesterday a soldier here shot himself. He was ready for the front but did not want to go. He was married and has two children.

There is a note in the papers that England has offered a large sum of money if anyone can take the Duke of Brunswick a prisoner so the Kaiser has forbidden him to go to the field again. I do not believe it at all.

We are badly in need of rain for we have had none for a long time.

Monday - Wednesday 7th - 9th June.

The Germans are confident that this month sees all Russians out of Austria.

We are desperately in want of rain. There was only one day of rain in the early part of May and all things are drying up. The heat is intense. This past two days it has been thirty degrees in the shade and no signs of rain.

Fraulein Ernst was here yesterday and she says that her brother writes from Austria for food. The food is so scarce and bad there with only one meal a day in the evening. And he is in the shooting graves! He writes that if he lives to be a hundred he would never forget Whit week of 1915. In terrible heat he marched two hundred kilometres in three days in full rig out. He then went directly into the shooting line, poor fellow. He has been wounded twice and this is his third time out.

I have applied for leave to go to Woltershausen for a short time. I am not at all well. It will take two weeks to get permission. The heat and dust is so stifling that I can scarcely breathe.

Today all the butchers have the order to only open half a day. Fresh meat is so scarce.

In the papers it states that if the harvest is not good then we cannot hold out this coming winter. But if anything can do it, it is the marvellous organisation. From the third month of the war everything eatable has been controlled. Germany knows to a day how long she can last.

America's sharp note is commented on in the paper and that all she says is all untrue. No one tells the truth but Germany.

Arthur writes me that he is surprised that my people do not write oftener because all their letters come through to him.

Saturday 12th June

I had a visit from Miss Seales, the Californian lady who is with Miss Marhgraf, and she is in a fix about cash and has had none for four months from America. At least I could help. Still a great deal of uneasiness over the American note.

Belle went to Celle today for a few weeks and I shall miss her terribly but Carole Osthaus has promised to write me any German letters that are necessary.

Wednesday 16th June.

We read today that England sank the under sea boat **U14** on the 8th of June but it has only been announced in small type. We never hear of a German boat being lost and one thinks that the English navy is asleep.

It is announced that the Ambassador who was sent to America regarding the sinking of the **Lusitania** has returned. But he is not at liberty to say anything to the press.

Belle used to take Arthur her bread allowance. She heard from the police today that her bread was now withheld in Hildesheim and she must have it in Celle. It is to prevent the people here getting her share whilst she travels.

Next month only so much fresh meat is to be bought on the same lines by ticket from the police. One must admire the organisation, it is so perfect. German soldiers, who have been sent into Austria to help, soon remark on the want of organisation there. The Austrians are very neglect in comparison with Germany.

Thursday 17th June.

I got my allowance to travel to the estate so I go on Monday .

There is news in the paper of bombs being dropped over Hull and of a great deal of damage being done. They also tell of forty French flyers being over Karlsruhe and dropped bombs on the streets there. Eleven civilians have been killed and fifty have been wounded.

Belle had a letter last Saturday from a friend in London (German) and he says that all Germans have orders to leave England. He has been naturalised for twenty years and feels it a great injustice. He is hoping to get leave to stay. I wonder if we will have to leave also.

Still no rain and the land is now parched. We have had no rain for seven weeks and we want it badly.

Friday 18th June.

Our John's birthday.

I read of the death of Edmund Lax in Austria. He was only at the front for one month and had been training soldiers here for seven months. He was a great friend of Arthur's.

I had a visit from the Californian lady yesterday. She is anxious over America and wants to get away. I am very sorry for her. She had a very unpleasant experience on her last visit here to me. On leaving me a man from the town saw her on the station in Hildesheim and evidently thought that she was an

Englishwoman. He went and gave information to a soldier (there are always a lot at the stations) that she was English and that they must see if she had permission to travel and what her business was. She was very indignant about it but it did no good. I told her that if I go further than three miles from here I must have permission from the police. They will give me a piece of paper saying that I am to go to such a place and what my business is. That paper I must hand to any person who asks me for it, civil or otherwise. If I do not have such a paper and I am more than three miles from here I can be marched off to prison by any person. And mind you, the civil people do it. They think they are helping their country.

A case in point. The place where Belle lives is very large and has perhaps thirty people living there in pension. A couple of weeks ago there came a stranger and she was a decent woman who kept herself to herself. Because the people in the place could not get to know anything of her (the manageress kept her mouth closed) one of the people privately went to the police and informed them. She thought she was a spy and asked them to enquire into it. They thanked her for being so very careful about her country and informed her that the manageress had already been there to announce her. This must be done with every single person who comes to sleep a night in the town. They said that they knew all about her and even told of the woman's private business to this creature. They explained she was a visitor and was to be married but her intended was at the front etc. etc. <u>Once more - organisation</u>.

There is not a soul in this town that they do not know all about.

Sunday 20th June.

Still no rain and things are looking serious for the crops and the potatoes are dying in the ground.

I hope this week to get permission to travel to the estate for a month or so as Hildesheim is too low for me. I must have stronger air and live much higher up.

I had a letter from Fraulein Lesdorff, she is in Salzdetfurth for the baths, and having heard that I was still here she has written to me to join her. But as I have applied for a permit to travel to Woltershausen this cannot be done. She is a fine old lady who I met at the baths six years ago and she goes there each summer and has been going for seventeen years. They are very strong salt baths and she says that they set her up for the whole year. She is seventy-six-years-old.

Tuesday 22nd June.

I go today to the estate and my permit will be ready. Dr. Myer has ordered me to take a course of baths for my heart. So on his orders I have got permission to travel twice a week into Bad Salzdetfurth to bathe and once a week into Hildesheim to visit him. This has been a long sickness. It is all heart and nerves and I shall not be better until the war is at an end. For that is the worry at the bottom of it all.

Wednesday 23rd June. Woltershausen.

I came here yesterday after a few disappointments. All my papers are in order but I dare not travel a mile from here without them. The police begged me not to go in the forest alone as people's tempers are not to be trusted.

I live with Hermenia Stoffegan; she was my cook for a couple of years, and thoroughly understands me.

Sunday 27th June.

The weather is perfect and I feel so much better here and I sleep so well. In the hotel if I slept two hours at once I thought that I had done well. Here I go to bed at half-past nine and sleep until three o'clock so that is a great improvement. One learns to be thankful for small mercies. I have brought my bread card with me and Hermenia gets me a little white bread but they must give up a lot of roggen (rye) for it. Here they eat only rye but I cannot digest it at all and the doctor has strictly forbidden it. It was an impossibility to buy white in Hildesheim for the baker dare not sell it. Even here the miller dare not grind wheat alone and he must put so much potato, meal, and so much rye amongst the wheat. Most people are ill with the bad bread.

Thursday 1st July 1915.

I have been here a week and am a little better. I keep losing flesh but that does not matter for I was much too stout. I must not lose too much says the doctor. I now weigh nine-and-a- half stones but sleep a lot better. The baths are doing me good but the first few took the use out of my hand (the old complaint).

I went into Hildesheim yesterday to see the doctor and he says I must stay here as long as I can and when the time is up (I applied for a month) we will apply for a longer period.

I am busy with the fruit and am canning a lot for the winter. I am also making jam and juice for my own use.

I have decided to take rooms and live private in the winter if Arthur is not with me. Please God this war is over by then though the English papers say no. It will last two years. Poor Arthur if he must spend two years in that awful place. He writes each week and last week we cut him a large box of cherries. The fruit is fine this year. I shall have two or three hundredweights of currants and at least ten stones of raspberry. Grapes are very full and cherries and pears are fine but the apples are worm eaten. That comes from the dryness.

Sunday 4th July.

I had a letter from Mr. Ralph of Stockport. He was here this time last year and all the people here now say that he was a spy. I was pleased to think he remembered me. He offered to send me anything he could but it is not allowed that I receive anything. I said he might send Arthur some tea and biscuits. It costs half a mark (six pence) to send a letter to England and I must buy a coupon (three pence) at the post office and enclose it in my letter which must be opened. I must address the letter and enclose it in an envelope to The Hague (Holland) and it is read there by the Germans and with the coupon a stamp is bought and then it goes away.

Dad wrote to me and it took five weeks for me to get it. Before the war it was thirty-six hours.

Monday 26th July.

Yesterday was my birthday and I cried all day. Hermenia remembered it and made quite a feast day of it. When I got in my sitting room I could not understand all the beautiful flowers. I had forgotten all about it.

Hermenia had fixed up the table and put two lovely roses on my plate. Then Henri sent a bunch and August (he is here on leave) and Frau. Steffregan sent me a large cake and more flowers. When I was having my breakfast two little children came in with more flowers. It upset me awful. That shows how my nerves have run down.

Arthur wrote me a nice long letter – he always writes very cheerful.

Now we are a nice family party. Hermenia's sister Anna is here with three bonnie children. A little girl Ruth, five-years-old, and a boy Fritz, three-years-old, (a regular little monkey) and a dear little baby Jean who is just like our little Bobbie in Castleton. He is so fat and so good tempered.

Then there is August the younger son of Steffregan's who is an under officer and is home for ten days on leave. He has been all the time in France by Verdun and he tells some dreadful tales of warfare. Anna is to stay one month and I am so glad. I take the baby out in a little cart and am very happy with him. He knows me and will come to me even from his mother. I have the little girl to sleep with me as there are two beds in my room and she occupies one. I have slept well ever since she came as the company is so good for me.

I hear very little of the war as the people in the village do not trouble much about it. It is only when one of our own people is killed or wounded that you hear much. If you hear of a great victory then they talk of it. But most is talk of the crops and animals.

All grain and animals have been reckoned. The government know to a few hundredweight what grain they will get. Early in the year a census was taken of the fields and each farmer must say how many acres he worked and how it was planted - so many acres wheat, barley, rye, hay, potatoes, swedes etc. At the threshing a man comes and takes account of how many hundredweight you have and then tells you how much you can have for yourself. You are allowed so much per head for your cattle and so much per head for yourselves according to the people in the house. Less than one-year-old does not count and from one to three you get half the amount. You get so many potatoes and four pounds of corn each week for each person and there is six ounces of bread per person and no more.

Many people do not have enough. They tell you that you must make vegetable soup and eat it twice a day. You are given a card to take to the miller and it comes from the mayor of the village. The miller dare not grind you more than so much a month. The baker dare not bake you more than so much bread a week as you have a card for him also. These bread cards are given out each month and you give them up every time you go to the miller or baker. You cannot bake in the houses here as they are the old fashioned stoves. Also yeast is forbidden to be sold and if you do get a little flour you cannot bake it. We have tried baking powder but it is not like yeast.

There was a notice in the papers this spring saying that no one must plant flower gardens but must grow vegetables and eat them to save bread. Now you often see peas, cabbage, beet etc. in the front gardens. Also more potatoes must be planted and not so much sugar beet. We can live without sugar says the notice. Every precaution is taken against hunger and people roast corn for coffee and it is very good. We roast it brown and grind it like coffee and it tastes alright.

It is a fine time for the farmer as all things are twice the price and the government pays market price for all. Of course, here in Germany, the government fixes the price and no one dare charge more but the government does pay the same price themselves. Henri Stoffregan reckoned up last week that a large farmer here who rents over a thousand acres has his rent alone in the money he received from his barley.

Monday 16th August.

We are quiet again. Anna and the children have returned to Leipzig and August has gone back to the front in France. He wrote yesterday and he and his regiment must go to Italy. He said when he was here that there were not enough soldiers of any great worth (in numbers) in France as they were building the places for the large guns. When they got to Warsaw they would remove a deal of artillery to France from Russia and then the war was only a question of a few weeks. If they could get a few more regiments in France it would soon end all.

I have been very busy in the garden but now it is very wet. The rain has come at last and seems to have come to stay. It grieves me to see our beautiful garden so neglected. Help cannot be got and the trees and bushes are just like a forest in the park land. The fruit garden is full of weeds but the fruit is fine. The vegetable garden is oats and potatoes. I shall have about fifteen tons of potatoes and the oats will buy me about seventy marks. The garden is about four acres but one acre is orchard. It is a pity about the fruit as I cannot get it to the station so it cannot be disposed of.

I send Arthur each week ten pounds of the food by post.

Wednesday 18th August.

We hear of Warsaw being taken and the people say that the war with Russia will end in six weeks. When Germany has taken the ring of fortresses all will be over. Certainly they are making progress hand over fist.

The Russian prisoners here will not believe it. We have in the place all told thirty-six Russian prisoners who must work on the land. They are fine big fellows and understand the land work. They get enough bread and so much potatoes and meat each day and sleep in a high barn. They get three-and-a- half pence a day pay and they like to do it. They think Germany is a beautiful place and only for being prisoners would like to live here. One of the men, as a prisoner, came through his native village on his way here and not a place was standing. He could not even locate where his house had stood. All was in ruins. He has a wife, his little ones and his mother. He cannot hear a word of them and sensitive he sits and cries. His comrades are very kind to him. They do not all work for one farmer as they are given out in six or eight to each farm.

One day when I was in Salzdetfurth I saw a train full of French prisoners come in. They are to work in the Kali works. These are mines, like our coal mines, and they are very short of men there. The French are not as big as the Russians but they are more active and seem very intelligent. Some of them seem to be of a better class family. One was a perfect gentleman to look at and his clothes were of the finest.

Sunday 22nd August.

I have received permission to stay here until October. Doctor said it was necessary and then will I go to live in the villa in Wörth Strasse Hildesheim. The villa is empty in October and in wartime it is too large to let so I have decided to live there. It will give me something to do to get it in order. There will be a comfortable place for Arthur to go when he is free. I have sold a great quantity of furniture but still have enough for five or six rooms. Belle will come to live with me so I shall not be so lonely.

I must get a little more flesh says the doctor. I have gone down to eight-and-a- half stones and that's too little. He says that I have to drink plenty of good red wine. And I dislike it so.

I have been busy this week putting vegetables in cans for the winter and making fallen apples into jelly. I am looking forward now to going in my own home again. Nine months of hotel life is enough to sicken one.

Sunday 29th August.

It is Hermenia's birthday so we are very happy. She had such a big post and I think it pleased her mother more than her to hear the letters read.

The people here seem to realise now that I do not intend to return. They cannot understand that we leave such a beautiful home and especially when we have spent so much money on it. One old man grumbled at me for an hour last week when I said that I could not live among such people. He said that we could live here all our lives and no one would molest us again. He said that the people had found out their mistake. The real truth is that they are afraid that a person will come into our house and work the land himself and then they will not have enough land for themselves. I asked the old man if we should consider the people who had not considered us. And if he thought that we must stay here just because the people thought it fit to let us. Then if they thought it fit to annoy us again they could do so.

I said it was not my character to live on tolerance and that wherever we lived it would cost money. For that money we could live anywhere. It was easy to find better people than lived in this village. The next day he sent a man to say that he had heard of a cheap motor car that would just suit Herr Dröege since we had now no horse. He does not believe, even yet, that we shall not return.

I hear very little about the war. They say that Italy makes no progress at all. But Belle says she reads in the neutral papers that they have got one or two large cities. The Germans say they got a lot of war material in the last place they took in Russia. I do not believe half I hear.

Tuesday 31st August.

I wonder when they will write from home. Their letters are very few and I long for news from Canada. I never hear from them at all. I had a letter from Gladys Unquhart last month and she says that she is now in the confectionery business as all things are bad on account of the war.

We received orders last week that all copper and brass must be given up to the government. All kettles and pans are being taken away and the people must get iron ones. It means a lot of trouble here. All the wash boilers are copper and when they cook a pig they cook it in the boiler. Here in our house the boiler is of copper and we can cook four hundredweights of plums at once as it is so large. The government will get a lot of copper that way but the people do not want to part with their heirlooms. Silver was collected early in the year and still gold is collected. In one place they received over eight hundred wedding rings and the people got the value in money and an iron ring in exchange. All the men here wear wedding rings so there is a great many in use.

The third war loan is called up at five percent interest and to be paid back in twenty years.

I had a long talk with Anna, the married sister of Hermenia who lives in Leipzig. She told me that she was often without bread in the house and could not buy it for love nor money and must cook potatoes often in the day.

I wonder if English prices compare with ours here.

Bread is two pence per pound, white bread four pence per pound, and limited to half a pound per day. Butter is two shillings per pound. Tea is eight shillings per pound. Coffee is two shillings and sixpence per pound. Meat for boiling is one shilling and three pence per pound. Meat for roasting is one shilling and ten pence per pound.

Lard is one shilling and sixpence per pound. Rice is a shilling per pound. Sago is ten pence per pound. Potatoes are one penny per pound. Milk is four pence per quart. Cream is forbidden to be sold. Oil is sixpence per quart. You can only get a quart per week and most houses burn lamps. Coal is one shilling and sixpence per hundredweight. Brickettes are one and three pence.

Many things you cannot buy and wooden articles are very scarce.

The English are to blame for it all.

You go each week to the town hall for your bread tickets. They have your name and address and how many people in the house. You get bread tickets accordingly. The baker dare not sell without these tickets because he must give tickets to account for his flour or his flour is short. When a stranger comes in he must bring his ticket from his town hall and take it to our town hall. He then gets it exchanged for one of ours or he gets no bread. You can only buy a dinner of vegetables and meat at a hotel. If you want tea and bread you must give your bread card – green tickets for four ounces and red tickets half a pound and so on. There is no way of dodging. If you are a farmer and have pinched a cut of corn the miller dare only grind you so much per month according to the people on your ticket, which is from the police. The baker dare only bake so much per week so you are stuck.

The worst is where there are children who always want a piece of bread. Here in the land it is better. The people have killed their two or three pigs in the winter and put them in cans. That is such a good idea.

One man in the village has a machine and sells the cans. A two pound can costs three pence and you cook your meat, vegetables and fruit, put it in the can and take it to the man. He puts a lid on, puts it in the machine, turns the handle for a second, and your lid is fixed on air tight. The Steinoffs killed a calf last week and the flesh was put in cans, eight and ten pounds, ready for the threshing feast. It's a fine idea. Then when you open the can it can be used again. You send it to the man with the machine and he cuts it level. The same can is used many times a year until it gets cut down too small for further use.

I have done twenty-two pounds of apples and twenty-six pounds of beans ready for the winter and then I will send them to Wörth Strasse villa. I will also send five hundred pounds of potatoes in sacks and two hundred pounds of apples and pears before I leave here.

Wednesday 1st September 1915.

I am glad August is over. The Germans have made great progress and so many forts in Russia have fallen. Over half a million prisoners have been taken. The papers each day are full of victories. Last August it was the same in France and Belgium.

I was in Hildesheim today and got a shock when I went to buy a few things. Woollen shirting, which I gave one shilling and nine pence per yard for in England and which was two shillings and nine pence here before the war, is now four shillings and nine pence per yard. They told me that when they sold out of their present stock there was to be no more.

The decorator, who I wanted to do some painting, told me that he could only do a little as his oil and turpentine was nearly run out and he could get no new. Oil that cost eight pence before the war was now two shillings and nine pence for the same quantity.

There are notices in the paper of the calling in of the half pieces of nickel (five pfennigs). We are to have them made out of iron and the nickel is to be used for bullets.

I think that things are bad for everyday we have men here to buy the animals and none are for sale. The price now is one hundred and twenty-five marks or shillings per hundredweight for pigs and one farmer was offered one hundred and forty shillings a hundredweight for a pig that weighed four hundred pounds. He refused it. So it sounds as if pigs are scarce.

I have enjoyed a good servant and Hermenia will come with me.

Arthur writes that he has hopes of being with me soon. I have my doubts.

They certainly have a way here of making you feel important. Just take the instance of my getting permission to travel to the estate, some twenty-eight miles distance, and going to take baths in Salzdetfurth which lies just between the two places, Hildesheim and Woltershausen. In the first place it took fourteen days to get permission and then I must announce to the mayor of the village that I was here by police permission. The police in Salzdetfurth were informed that I came to bathe three times a week and the railway officials too. The man who owns the baths was also informed that I was coming. The officials on our rail (Woltershausen) were informed that I could travel three times a week and the railway servants in Hildesheim also. All my letters must go to the Hildesheim police to be read before they go away and before I receive them. It is enough to make you feel <u>very</u> important.

We are having miserable weather this last few weeks and it is bad for the farmers.

Saturday 4th September.

We hear that all the fortresses of Russia have fallen and that there is to be a big transport of men and guns to France.

In the papers today there is a list of what people can do to help their government to have plenty to give the people to eat. With two million prisoners there will be a lot to do to provide food. Every rood of German land has been cultivated. Where there were no men to work the land prisoners have been sent. They are to gather all the horse chestnuts to cook for the pigs, and all acorns. Parties of school children go and gather them. All cherry stones (from preserving), all plum stones and all small nuts from the lime trees are to be gathered and sent to be made into oil. Very good oil is in the nuts and the people can cook with it.

Every school has so much used wool and cotton yarn sent according to the numbers of scholars (girls) and the school is responsible for so many socks for the soldiers. The management is fine and the little ones knit the legs and the older ones knit the feet. The children must take the work home and do so much per week.

Friday 10th September.

Went to Hildesheim today and arranged for the house. Belle is quite excited and takes such a great interest in it. I am sure that we will be happy there - as much as we can be in these times. I am feeling a lot better and I notice it in the walk to and from the station. Before I had to rest many times because of palpitation but now I rest only once.

They are taking in all the copper, brass and nickel this week. Belle went into a shop to buy a piece of nickel and they said they dare not sell any metal other than enamel. In the drapers also only one bobbin of cotton is allowed to each person. Belle had asked for two.

If you take your brass pans, candlesticks, copper kettles etc. before the 20th of September you get one shilling and sixpence a pound for brass, two shillings for copper and ten shillings for nickel. After the 20th it is to be called up. Then it has not been given free willing and you will only get one third the price. They have a way here of making you free willing.

The gendarme called here yesterday and told them to get their iron kettles ready. For if they had killed a pig, and the copper kettles were called up, they would have nothing to cook it in.

There is ammunition for over twelve months. Germany always looks twelve months ahead.

After next week we are to have more bread per person as the harvest has been good and we were only limited to see if the harvest was all right. Even if it was not we have bread enough on this allowance until next year's harvest is ready.

I went hay making yesterday and we are having lovely weather.

Had a letter from James Walmsley and he says that there is a record August in Blackpool and all our people are there. He says Winnie has grown in the last twelve months.

Here in Germany there are no bands or amusements and never a piano in a house is played. Everyone is too serious and all have people at the front and nearly all have lost someone. Sadness is the chief note. No one thinks of pleasure trips and they cannot believe it is not the same in England. When I mention it they wonder at the want of feeling displayed. According to our papers they are terribly afraid of a German invasion in England.

Wednesday 15th September.

We are sad today for the last son of the Stoffregans must go away tomorrow and he is the third son to go.

The old man is too old to plough it and the wife and daughter are very much upset.

We had news yesterday that we can have no more butter for the next few days and the people are angry about it. Butter and milk are scarce at the dairies and the people say that if they get no butter they will keep their milk and make butter themselves. I cannot understand it for we always got our butter from Holland.

Yesterday, and also last Sunday, from every pulpit the people were begged to take up the third war loan. If you pay ninety-six marks you get papers for a hundred marks before the 20th of September. But if it is later you must pay the hundred marks for a hundred worth of paper. The people are told to take all their savings out of their saving banks and put it in the loan. They will get five percent and can always sell their certificates if necessary. If the people do not quite understand about it then they must go to their Catholic or Protestant priest and he will do all the correspondence for them. The smallest sum is one hundred marks or five pounds sterling.

We are having lovely weather this September and I am busy with the fruit and am out all day. I feel extra well. Belle and Carole are coming tomorrow so I am preparing for them a little.

My stay here is drawing to a close. I go to Hildesheim early in October.

Thursday 16th September.

We had a nice day on Tuesday and Carole and Belle were delighted with the place. We had a long chat with Stoffegan about the prices of pigs which are now at one hundred and fifty marks (shillings) per hundredweight. Swine flesh is one shilling and ten pence per pound, beef two shillings, butter two shillings and two pence, flour four pence, lard one shilling and eight pence, rice one shilling and eggs two pence each. Many things are too dear for the poor people to buy and many are not to be had. Coal is one shilling and ten pence per hundredweight and coke is one shilling and six pence for the same.

Carole took her metal things to the call up and told me that she took six bronze candlesticks and got more money for them than they cost twenty-five years ago.

Frau Pastor met us going to the station. She had been to Hildesheim to buy a few things for the winter. She had bought shoes for her son William, similar to the ones I had bought for Arthur last November and had cost me twenty-eight shillings, and they were now sixty-five shillings a pair.

We read that the military are to have shoes for the winter with wooden soles and leather uppers. The people are advised to buy them also. Leather is so short.

We had a letter yesterday from a son of the Stoffregans, brother to Hermenia, and he has a new address and he says that they are waiting for new guns as they lost all theirs on the 8th of this month. Most of his friends were taken prisoners and twelve were shot dead. He has luck has Detrick. He has now twice escaped capture by a very small item.

No war news of any note just to say each night, "Making progress in all directions". But it never says how much.

The fruit is ripe now and I am very busy during the day. I feel very well again as this air is so pure.

Sunday 26th September.

My stay here is getting short and I leave on the 10th or 11th of October. I am busy now getting the house in Wörth Strasse in order.

I had a letter from Arthur saying that he dreads the coming winter for last winter he lived under such very bad circumstances. Also his cough, which he has not had for four years, has returned. I must make him some chest preservers.

I planted our garden (we have three acres of vegetable garden) with oats and potatoes and for the oats I get fourteen shillings and sixpence a hundredweight and for the potatoes I get four shillings a hundredweight. So I have done very well. The fruit is rather difficult to sell and the pear trees are so full. All corn has been called up by the government and you are allowed to keep nine pounds a week for each person and for horses you are allowed three pounds of oats a day. For other cattle you must buy from the miller who gets it from the government. All prices are fixed and eggs must not be more than two pence each and so on. It's a good idea as it prevents one person buying more than another.

Frau Pastor took her brass and copper kettles, candle-sticks etc. last week and she got seventy-two marks for them. Some have been in the family for a hundred years.

The third war loan is overpaid as everyone has put money into it.

I am much better and go for my last kohlensäure bath next week and have gained two pounds in two weeks.

I have had no news from my people for over two months. <u>It's too bad.</u> It makes me wonder if there is bad news and they will not write it.

Sunday 3rd October 1915.

We are having lovely weather and the harvest is all in and only a few potatoes are left in the fields. Today is Harvest Thanksgiving so all are at church.

I went to Hildesheim yesterday to arrange about the boiler going away. It is copper and all copper is called up. With so many being called up at once the iron boilers fail for the workers are scarce and you must wait three or four weeks before the copper boiler is replaced.

A police officer called and told me that our house is large enough for six soldiers in quartering so I am sure of having two. Hildesheim has so many military there.

Grebe the agent for the property was here Monday last and said that he could not get half the rent and some people said that they must give up the land for their men fail and they cannot work it themselves.

It is a dreadful time for the poor people and now they are limited to butter at so much per person, as lard and dripping are not to be got. You can go to six or eight shops for flesh and fat and get not one ounce. We have made a lot of jam but it is not good to eat too much. Still it is better than nothing.

Belle came to me with a Frau Degenhart and her sister and the Frau D. would like our place for her son. They were delighted with everything around it.

Sunday 10th October.

It is decided that I go tomorrow to Hildesheim and Hermenia goes with me. I don't know whatever I should have done without her. Her great kindness I will never forget. I go to the hotel after a few days until the house is in order. The furniture comes on Wednesday and

I hope to be soon in order. It has been very hard to get workmen. In fact there is no light in the house yet and oil is so scarce that you are only allowed one quart per household per month. The plumber also fails us and we cannot tell when he comes for all people want gas putting in their houses on account of the scarcity of oil. I can see us being upset for a long time. Thank goodness the painter and decorator is able to come though we cannot have any oil paint for the oil fails. I have had water colour put in one room and it looks very nice.

Saturday 16th October.

I went yesterday to Woltershausen as I had a permit until the 15th just to say goodbye to a few. I shall not be allowed more than two and a half miles away after today.

The furniture is in my house and two rooms are in order. I am glad Belle is in Celle for we are so plagued with workmen and I should like her rooms to be in order before she comes back. If only we had light. I am very comfortable in the hotel and Herr and Frau Roeder are very kind to me but I am anxious to be settled in my own home.

Tuesday 19th October.

Hermenia came yesterday to stay a few days with me so we've slept in the house for the first time. We got some oil so we were able to use the lamp. It is surprising how many houses have no light - only oil here. Houses at thirty and forty pounds rent a year with no gas or electricity! This town is fifty years behind one of its size in England. Many houses of fifty pounds a year rent do not have bathrooms and it is only this past three or four years they have water closets. Thank goodness we have both.

Monday 25th October.

We have been very busy this past few days and we are as far in order as it is possible to be for we are only waiting for the men. The new girl came on the 20th. Hannah is her name and she seems a good worker and pleasant. But she can't cook. Hermenia is here yet so it does not matter.

Today we have our first frost and it is very cold with five degrees of frost. There is every promise of a long and severe winter. <u>God help the poor soldiers in the field.</u>

Wednesday 27th October.

I had a letter from Alice Graeinghoff, Mrs. Durselen's daughter, from Königswinter. She and her husband are in Berlin and Herman is using his influence to pay Arthur a visit. I also received yesterday a parcel of old clothes from Arthur and a parcel with tea and biscuits. It was such a welcome surprise and it gave me great pleasure.

I also received a letter this morning from Arthur and it made me so sad. I am afraid that he is ill. Or losing his hopes and that is just as bad. Though it is a long time since we met, eleven-and-a- half months, still we must live in the hope of it coming to an end. But when one is not well things look so very black all round.

Thursday 28th October.

Our Ettie's birthday.

Received a letter also a wire from Alice Graeinghoff and Herman has permission to visit Arthur on Friday

29th. How very delighted he will be. I hope that it is a long visit and not just a few minutes. They promise to come for a visit on their return so we can have a long chat.

Hermenia had to return yesterday as her mother is not so well. I am sorry. Still, the maid shapes very well.

Saturday 30th October.

Grebe the agent for the land sent for me yesterday. He has had notice that he must give an exact account of all my belongings, the estate, monies etc. so I have left all in his hands.

Belle came home yesterday and is very pleased with her rooms and they are very comfortable. She has had a nice time with Rosie in Celle for three weeks.

Tuesday 2nd November

The Graeinghoffs came today and leave tomorrow. Herman tells me that he saw Arthur for three quarters of an hour but of course four soldiers were in the room. Arthur looks well but thin, and seems to be in good spirits. He tells Herman that he is constantly busy and I am glad to hear it. It must have been a very difficult task to obtain permission to visit. Herman tells me that he was three whole mornings visiting various officers before he got permission to visit the General Commander and state his wish. I had written to Königswinter to say I was afraid Arthur was ill because of a letter I had received. That was the ground that Herman obtained permission to visit Arthur.

We are told today that all pfennigs (they are made of copper and about as large as a three penny bit) are to be called up for bullets and we are to have them made of iron.

I received also a letter from Ettie and she says that they have had such a lot of letters returned. I cannot understand it as I get letters from friends much more often.

Friday 5th November.

I have such worrying thoughts about our Kittie in Canada and last night I had such awful dreams and she was in every one and in such trouble. It does worry one especially as I have no news of her.

From the 1st of November all meat shops have been closed for three days a week and the restaurants dare not cook any meat, or the lodging houses, on two days a week. When we do have meat allowed we are not to fry or roast it but boil it to save the fat being wasted. It is so very dreadful to get any fat to cook with and we get fat cards now with the bread cards and no one is allowed to sell to a person without a card. These we get every week from the giving out offices. We are allowed half a pound of bread per person per day and quarter of fat, either bacon or lard, per person per <u>week.</u>

When you have cooked a quarter of bacon fat you can eat it once, but you can fry three times in a quarter of lard. It's to make it last longer but it's rotten to keep house on. Just imagine no meat at all for three days and two out of the remaining four you are only to eat boiled stuff. That is five days a week without fat.

Butter you are allowed to buy without cards, when you can get it and it costs three shillings and three pence a pound. It is very scarce and so is milk for we have the foot and mouth disease as well as a shortage of cattle. I get fits when I go out shopping as prices change so quickly and are always higher. I wonder if on November the 1st they are paying in England four pence a pound for white bread, three shillings and threepence for butter, one shilling and eleven pence for lard, one shilling and nine pence for margarine, a shilling for rice, six shillings for tea, two shillings and nine pence for roasting beef, one shilling and ten pence for boiling, pork two shillings and four pence, ham two shillings and sixpence, bacon two shillings and a penny, and eggs at three pence each. Most things in the household are double the price. Soap is at one shilling and a penny a pound, candles three pence each and matches at sixpence a dozen boxes.

On November 5th all prices are to be set fast by the government so perhaps they will be cheaper and then they cannot make them any higher. Anyone selling above this price will get twelve months imprisonment and their place of business will be closed. One man had six months imprisonment (no fines) for doing something like that and his place of business closed up.

Monday 8th November.

Now there are new rules as regards drink. You can only buy spirits during certain hours with none to be sold after nine o'clock at night and to no householder. You must sit in a hotel and drink what you buy. You cannot take a drop home. I wanted three pence worth of rum for cooking and it was not to be got for love nor money.

We were in a shop today and a man came in to order champagne and asked for a French brand. The owner said that he had a few bottles but during the week the police had been there and counted what he had and he was forbidden to sell any of it. The maker of that brand, a Frenchman, had said something insulting of the Germans so not a drop of his champagne must be sold. I think that is cutting off your nose to spite your face. The champagne is lying in the cellar and that is as good as money lying there. But one does not understand things and perhaps there is another motive for it all.

I have received during the week a newspaper and one letter and they have been in Köln for fourteen months. The paper is of August 2nd 1914 and the letter July the 30th and though so old were very welcome.

There is an announcement in the papers asking the people not to do all their work themselves. But to leave some for after the war as so many poor men will come back and require labour. They certainly do look ahead here.

Today when I went to report to the police a mother was dragging her boy in because he had been naughty. Here the police see to them for, as they say, the fathers are away at the front and someone must control them and women are not fit to look after boys. He did howl and was terrified when taken in the police room. You are summoned by the police here for the smallest thing.

It is sometime this week that the eighteen-year-olds are called up. The soldiers one meets in the streets are wonderful and so many. But they are not the fine looking men that were here at first. Many have been wounded once, twice, and three times and some have gone back for the fifth time into the field. It seems strange to see soldiers with dark blue glasses and one or two have such bad coughs. Our plumber has been called away. He has a glass eye and never thought he would be called.

Sunday 14th November.

Had Carole and Rosie v.d. Busch here to tea and supper and it was very nice and comfortable.

We read in the papers that after this month all small change will be given in postage stamps. For instance when we go into a shop and give one shilling and want eight pence change we get one penny or half penny stamps. I wonder what it means. It's such a funny way of doing business. Why not have sixpence notes? We have had one shilling (mark) since the first week of the war and if you give ten shillings (paper of course) you get change, say nine shillings in paper. We have one, two, three and five shilling notes and they are so dirty.

Tuesday 16th November.

Elizabeth Day and it is a general holiday for she is the patron saint of Hildesheim. Protestant and Catholic have a general holiday and all the shops are closed. There are three masses, just as Sunday, in all the churches.

Arthur has written me a nice long letter and I have sent him a parcel. He says it is a long time since he has had anything from England so I must write to them. He reminds me that it is over twelve months since we were separated. But there is no need to remind me. Why? Because I cannot bear to think of it!

I had a letter from Alice Graeinghoff and one from Mrs. Durselen and she promises to visit me in the New Year. I have just filled in my paper with all the brass and copper and it is ready when called up. Such a lot has been given by the free willing that we hope for peace before ours is needed.

In the last fourteen days there has been great progress in Serbia, Nis has fallen, and it is the greatest fortress the Serbians have and each day we read of a few thousand prisoners. I got a 'Times' yesterday and read of the dreadful Armenian outrages but there was not a word in our papers. I should think it is a surprise to England that Nis has fallen so very quickly.

Last week a priest was arrested here. They think he is a spy. The poor man, he has had a time. First he was in Alsace Lorraine and was taken for a spy there, he is German, and so the French ill-used him. He came here for protection and after three months he is now in prison. Some dreadful tales are about.

Saturday 20th November.

I hear today that Canon Heiser, the old priest I used to confess to, is very ill and not expected too live. I am so very grieved for I am very fond of the old gentleman and I realise that I must get a new confessor and that is not so nice for me in a strange land. He spoke English so very well.

Belle says she reads in the paper that Leo Havermann (Arthur's cousin) is dead. It does not trouble me. I have nothing to thank him for. He was very unkind to me in my trouble for which I shall never forget. He thought that the world and God else was only for the Germans. Still I wish him a peaceful rest. He might have been kinder to a lonely woman in a strange land during war time.

We have the foot and mouth disease in many a village and it is a great pity for we were short of milk and butter before we got this disease.

The little children are all wearing wooden shoes for leather is not to be got at all. It makes such a noise to hear a crowd coming from school. So many of the children have a breaking out on their hands and faces, it seems to be a regular disease, poor blood I suppose. It is because the food cannot be nourishing as so much is potato food and the flour you buy is half potato meal.

Sunday 28th November.

Rosie is on a visit to me so being three we are very comfortable.

There is a notice in the papers about people laughing at the Landstorm men when they are drilling and is forbidding them to do it. I think it is a great shame for the most of the poor fellows have never been in the army having being exempt because of some ailment in their youth. Now they must all go out and fight. When one is forty-five-years-old one is not as able as the young ones. Also they are very stiff. Still it is dreadful of the people to laugh and I feel so sorry for them for they are mostly married and all look so very sad.

All red wine is to be confiscated on December 1st.

Wednesday 1st December 1915.

This week has been very cold and we have frost.

Arthur writes me that he has hopes of leave in early spring so he must have heard something of it.

Frau Mummers says that she has a son, a waiter in England, and he is imprisoned. His wife visits every week. Yet here it is not at all allowed.

Wednesday 8th December.

Not much to report only that there is a shortage of lard and there is to be no more until after Christmas. We have the cards but cannot buy it. Margarine is one shilling and eight pence per pound and can be got only by chance. If a shop gets a box of margarine there are crowds waiting for it.

Herr Grebe has announced all my goods. Each piece of silver, old furniture, jewellery, all monies, papers, properties etc. has been sent in. It has been a job.

Tuesday 14th December.

It is sad to read of Serbia and now all talk is of Egypt and the American note on Austria. I don't think anything will come of it. It was the same over the **Lusitania**.

There is an order that we give all our rubbish to the government. Soldiers are at every house this week with small carts for old rags, metal, paper, clothes boxes. Anything you have in the cellars, or attics, that is not in use must be given up. The mode of organisation is wonderful and not a scrap of anything is wasted here. I wonder if it is the same at home. Even the little children work for the government as much as they can. Every one does what they can to help, even the poorest ones. If such methods were in England then such a lot could be done at very little expense.

Thursday 16th December.

Today there is a notice and we are not to bake any cakes for Christmas as it is forbidden to use flour, yeast, eggs or fat of any description. We know that the cakes we buy are made of potato, meat, egg powder and baking powder.

There is also a notice that they are coming for the metal, copper and brass. That was announced in October so our wash kettle and brass candlesticks must go and then we will have enough ammunition for <u>six years.</u> I do hope the war will not last as long as that. I feel so often without any hope at all of an end to it.

Ny, (the butter woman), who comes here from the dairy tells me we are to have only a quarter pound of butter a <u>week</u> per person and we will have cards from the police just like the bread cards. That is very little when you think there is no cooking fat to be got at all. There seems to be a famine in fat.

One day this week there was a deal of grumbling in the market as regards food. They ask you at the post, when you send a parcel to the field, if there is fat of any kind in it because it is forbidden. The soldiers are not to receive any from home because they get fat in their food in the field.

It is forbidden to sell yeast at all to prevent the people from baking for fear they use eggs or lard and because some have a store from the summer. It is dreadful for poor people and they must have hunger at these prices.

A woman with one child only gets twenty-one shillings and sixpence a <u>month</u> from the government and often has quartered on her a soldier. If she is very poor she must go to the Red Cross Society and they often pay half her rent and give her a ticket for so much food. The husband in the field gets sixpence a day so he cannot send much home.

My quartering came on December 12th and it was two soldiers from the lazarett. They have been wounded in

Russia and now they are better they must return in a few weeks. I had made arrangements for them to sleep at a neighbour's and she gives them coffee in the morning and a vegetable soup in the evening. I pay nine pence for each man and she gets also one and a half pence a day from the government for each man. This woman's husband is in the field and she has two rooms ready for the soldiers.

Having six in all it pays her for one fire and one light is enough. But when you reckon that coal is two shillings a hundredweight and coke is one shilling and eight pence a hundredweight it is very dear firing. We are glad that they are so very comfortably off. They come here one night a week for supper and Hannah (the kitchen maid) has them in the kitchen and I send them a bottle of beer and a cigar each. One speaks English perfectly and the other has a good idea of it having learnt it at school. Both are very nice fellows and must come from good homes. They said to me: 'Don't worry about your husband being in Ruhleben. It's better than being in the field in winter. If he was free he would be in the military'.

I have felt it for a long time that of the two evils it is better as it is, for both bring anxiety.

Tea, coffee and cocoa are called up by the government and we are only allowed to have so much in our houses. Also milk is to be censored. In my opinion this all points to famine for the poor people.

The weather is cold but not as cold as in early December. Then we had twelve degrees of frost and many burst water pipes and no plumber to repair them. It is in these things that we miss the men. It is a great trouble to get any jobs done. I should like a lot of wood sent here from the estate but cannot get anyone to do the carting as both men and horses fail.

Such a poor lot of horses are on the streets and I feel so sorry for them. At the rate of food (three pounds of corn per day) they are simply a bag of bones. I remarked one day that: 'I have never in all my life seen such horses'.

The reply came: 'I never in all my life saw such a war as this'.

So it is with everything else.

Thursday 30th December.

I am glad it is the end of the year and we can at least wonder what the next will bring us. We can hope for better days even if we do not get them.

Arthur wrote me on the 18th saying that he had a pudding from Lily for Christmas and he was so pleased.

I heard nothing from home.

I am glad that Christmas is over. Belle and I spent it very quietly here. On one evening we went to Carole Osthaus and the next evening Carole and Fil Lebereuhn came to us.

The two soldiers came for supper on the 26th so I left them in the dining room for the evening with Hannah and the soldiers had a pleasant evening.

Belle and I went to the cathedral and then returned home and went to bed. I had to get up to go to the police (my daily visit) and then we had dinner and then another rest. That is how we spent Christmas. I thought the whole time of home and wondered how many were there together. It makes one sad when I think of the big parties we had only a very few years ago. And where we all are now - so scattered and so far apart. We should make as much as we can of Christmas for the time comes only too soon when it becomes a sad anniversary. But it gave me a certain amount of pleasure to look back on a few of the Christmases I have spent.

Wednesday 5th January 1916.

Now we are well in another year and I pray that it brings us peace.

Arthur has not written since the 18th of December but he said then that he hoped to be allowed to go to Berlin and pay a call for a couple of hours on his cousin Johanna Pulmann. I do not think that he got permission for one of them would have written.

Alice Graeinghoff has written and says that a friend of theirs has been exchanged for an English prisoner and that he is surprised at the bitterness he finds here. He says that he was well treated in the Handforth camp and the men exchanged have written to thank the English government for their treatment. It's good to read it. If only we could see the end.

The papers are full of conscription in England. Of course I do not know of what it is to consist. But if is anything like they have here, well, revolution is better in my opinion. But of course I get so little news that I can believe. For if you read one thing today it is contradicted in another day or two.

Yesterday I had a couple of friends to coffee. One has a sister in London and the other a brother in Australia. Both have not heard from them for some time and are full of anxiety.

I cannot understand the letters not coming. Surely the members of my family have not left me the whole of Christmas without even a thought to put on paper? It is announced in the papers here how to address a letter to

England to assure its safe delivery. Surely something of the kind is done in England to relieve the anxiety of relatives.

Today it is announced in the papers that we must tell how much weight of potatoes we have in the house over twenty pounds. Here in Germany everybody buys their potatoes by the hundredweight at the beginning of winter. I had six hundredweights sent here from the farm so I must announce all I have over the twenty pounds. It is so the government understands how many will be in hand when the new harvest is planted.

We are awaiting the new Income Tax every day and I have heard that the outlanders are to be heavier taxed than the Germans – we shall see.

Friday 7th January.

Lots of callers today as it is Belle's birthday. Every one of your friends calls and brings you good wishes and a flower or plant. Tomorrow she goes out to supper so I shall have a quiet evening.

I have not been so well again and had a bad heart attack so I am going to a heart specialist in a few days. I seem to be going like mother. My pains remind me so much of her. We will see what a good doctor can do.

Steinoff came last week and says that William goes this month to the military and he must apply for a prisoner to do his work.

Hermenia came to see me and says all is well at home. Frau and Herr Pastor wrote me their greetings – they are very kind indeed.

I also had a Christmas card from Miss Seales, the Californian lady that I helped to get to America. She is now safe and thanks me for letting her have the money. It's a pleasure to know one can be of help to someone in these bad times. She must be so glad to be amongst her own people again.

Tuesday 11th January.

It seems very strange to read today that the English have left Gallipoli after it having cost so much blood. But of course I only read it in these papers.

I have been ill again and went last week to a specialist and he ordered the 'Röntgen Rays' so I have been photographed today. I was dreadfully nervous but I think it will turn out well. I have no fear of cancer and think that it is all nerves. But the pain is a bit stiff at times and nothing relieves it. I am so thin at that. Perhaps it is an old ulcer breaking out again but I shall be glad when all is in order and I know what to expect.

Arthur writes me today that he has hopes of a visitor and that it will indeed be a day of joy when he sees me again. I daresay it will be even if it is only one hour in a crowded room. Ten days is the longest we have been apart since we were engaged and now it is fifteen months. Belle says it will teach us to have more regard for each other and may do us good. For my part it is an unnecessary lesson. I could have gone along without this and my fear is that this worry has done harm and unnecessarily shortened life. One never knows, it might be for the best. Or the opposite may come of it. I only know that if the present anxiety could be removed I would give all I have at the present moment. I daresay that there are plenty in the same boat.

Friday 14th January.

Received a letter from Arthur today and he has had permission to enclose one from Ettie. She sent it on the 30th of December and Arthur got it on the 11th of January. It did not take long.

Been to the doctor and he says most is nerves but my heart is enlarged. So I <u>must</u> be big hearted (what oh!).

We are filling up our papers for milk and potatoes. I have to say how many pounds I have in the house, how many people, and if they will last until the middle of July. Also how much milk I can manage on, give the age of us all, and say if milk is at all necessary through doctor's orders. If you have children under five-years-old you get milk for certain but not at all certain otherwise unless sickness is in the house.

I read today that the English have given up the Dardanelles. Here they have always made fun of the English stopping in such an impassable place. They criticise all the boasting speeches that the English have made.

Ettie says she thinks we shall be together next Christmas but I do not think so. For these past few months I seem to have lost all hope.

It is strange to see how the people are now willing to buy English preparations. The first months of the war they insulted you if you asked to buy them and now they tout them in their windows. They even have the English directions in them. I have bought salmon, cornflower, tea, whisky, soap and medicines, all English packed, this last week.

Sunday 16th January.

There seems to be unrest in the people today.

It is announced that the capital of Montenegro is in German hands and there is lots in the paper of conscription in England. Here they are glad it has come to pass so that the English will know what it is to be a servant to the government. If only they can bow the Englishman down to know servitude then they do not care.

The butcher told me today that meat will be very scarce in a month or so from now. And a friend said that there was a deal of people grumbling at the town hall about rice, sago etc. They publicly told the crowd that England had forbidden the neutral lands to sell Germany anything so they could starve her out. I said no neutral land dare refuse to trade with Germany because, if so, she was no longer neutral and had taken the side of the enemy. But they believe what the magistrate said. I think it is because Germany has no gold and that the neutral lands will not accept the paper money at all.

We also read of a breakfast being given by the Chancellor. The Kaiser was there and various members of the cabinet. It seems to me as if it has been a cabinet meeting, but not in name, with the War Minister, Finance Minister, and Chancellor etc. I wonder if we shall hear of anything that passed. If only it would bring peace.

Monday 17th January.

I had the enquarterings in to supper and they say that we shall soon have peace for the people of Montenegro have begged for freedom and it has a great political significance. Also that the Austrians have gained a high fortress that is the Gibraltar of the Adriatic Sea and England's flotilla is as good as done for as regards warfare. There is great jubilation over it and a certainty that peace is in the air.

I have been thinking a lot about Kittie and her little son. How strange it seems for so much to happen to ones nearest and dearest. All I hear is that Kittie is married and then that Kittie has a son. Is it two or three-weeks-old? I wish her luck with her little one from the bottom of my heart and would give a deal for a line from her. What a change this last two years has brought. But I know each day will be one nearer the end.

Tuesday 18th January.

Had very sad news today. This evening came a letter from Königswinter to say that Mrs. Durselen had dropped down dead at a coffee party in Ronsdorf where she was staying with her sister. It has upset me a deal. I had a letter from her only two days ago. What a sudden end and how very sad for the two girls, Lena and Emily in England, but it is a death she would have liked for she often told me that she did not want to lie in a sick bed and be any trouble to anyone. I look back with pleasure on her visit to me in 1914 when she spent seven weeks in Woltershausen. It will be a big shock to Alice Graeinghoff.

Friday 21st January.

Strange news in the paper. It reports that the Montenegro people deny that they are in want of peace. The papers say that they cannot say if it is true or not. We had made a great victory of it here and had all the flags flying. It's very strange and we must await further news.

It is such miserable wet weather with rain all day and yet so warm that the trees are in full bud and many rose trees are in leaf.

There is a new order that all children must be out off the streets at seven o'clock. It is because their fathers are not at home to make them obey and they are disobedient to their mothers. Also they do not learn any good in the streets running wild after seven o'clock. The mother is fined fifty pfennigs if it is her fault. Such as not being at home or not reporting a disobedient child to the police. If it is the child's fault he is punished by the police.

Here, as in England, January is devoted to an annual sale in all the shops but this year it has been forbidden by the government. Why is not told.

I bought some fish for dinner today at eleven pence a pound (cod) and I said that it was dear. The man said that we should be lucky if we got any at all next week for there had been less in the market every week this past two months. I do not know why, and the meat is very scarce.

Monday 24th January.

Had a letter from Alice Graeinghoff telling me that Mrs. Durselen's death was a stroke. She died at once after remarking 'I do feel bad' and she gradually sank to the floor. They thought she had fainted and ran to her assistance but she was dead. What a nice end for her. She had no pain at all, but how dreadful for the children. I feel so very upset over her and cannot get her out of my mind.

It is advertised today that all firms using steam or electric power are not to work their machines more than twenty-eight hours a week. But they are obliged to pay their workers the same wages as if they were working full time. Or at least the wages they were receiving in January 1915.

All the remnants of brass or copper have to be given up this month. Also the <u>walnut trees</u> must be chopped down because the government want the wood for guns. Rosie v.d. Busch writes from Celle that she has to give up her two trees. In a village near here over two hundred trees (walnut) are being cut down ready to go away. It is so sad to see them go. In some places they are planted all along the roadway for a couple of miles.

They report today that it is quite true about Montenegro but that England does not know it yet. The King of Montenegro is so angry with England that he has not even sent them word of his giving in. One does not know what to believe these days.

Wednesday 26th January.

Received a postcard from our Willie today. It is such a pretty photo of Joan and it did me good to see it.

Now we hear of the deceitfulness of King Nicholas of Montenegro. The papers do give it to him for his cunning. He has gone to France, so it says, but he is more a prisoner of England for they have sent a bodyguard of over sixty soldiers with him.

Such a lot of things are called up by the government and the lists of forbidden things (to sell) are every day announced, and each day it is more.

Friday 28th January.

Feel bad today. I wish I could get a little better.

It was the Kaiser's birthday yesterday and a great feast. There is a collection on Sunday in every church in Germany for the Kaiser's birthday gift and then he will give the various sums to the Red Cross or to the Soldier's fund etc.

Had a letter from Arthur and he says that they have had no answer to the petition for visitors. Still I have hope of it.

Herr Stoffregan was here on a visit today and tells me that the man Rutt, who accused us of being spies, met with an accident and was buried yesterday. I am sorry for him and his wife also as she is badly left with five children. Everyone thought it was him that cut our telephone wire. Well, poor fellow, he will cut no more.

I read in the papers that the English were once more 'too late' in getting somewhere in Albania. They have nicknamed them here '**too late nation**' and make great fun of them always being last.

Saturday 29th January.

We hear of mobilisation in Romania. I never expected that. How foolish of a nation to go into war if they can keep out. Here the war is felt very much as regards work and food. It's difficult to get the latter and there is great trouble over the butter. One wonders where it will all end.

Hannah Stoffregan has written from Leipzig and says she can only get a quarter pound of butter per week and it is three shillings and sixpence a pound and now fat bacon is three shillings a pound. Potatoes are not to be had, but it does not matter much for people all have them stored – we get them in sacks here.

It must be very bad for the poor people and especially those with children. One poor fellow I heard of today has lost one eye and an arm and he was in a good position before the war. He earned four pounds per week and now he has a pension of forty-five shillings per month and has a wife and three children. He will not be allowed to work any more. I do not know how they can exist at all.

It is stated that England is waiting to see what Germany is doing to her foreigners' properties before she taxes. We are still in suspense until it is settled.

We hear very little of the conscription act of England, just a report that it has been passed with a big majority. Single men are first and then married men up to thirty. I cannot think it is like the German conscription at all. But of course I do not know.

Wednesday 2nd February.

There is sad news in the paper today. We read of a terrible battle in the air over England on the night of January 31st. I myself cannot see how so much damage can have been done unless it is that England has no watchmen. They report that the airships, eight in number, went into Liverpool and spread death and destruction there and then on to Manchester. Sheffield and Nottingham were also surprised and though they shot at them the Luftships returned intact to German headquarters. According to these papers Manchester and Liverpool are in parts and are a heap of stones and 'the land of England is at last in the air flown'. I only half

House in Hildesheim

Country retreat in Bad Salzdetfurth

Home in Woltershausen

While I breathe, I hope

believe it. The last bombs were flung on Yarmouth and the Humber. The people here are very pleased and quite believe it.

Thursday 3rd February.

Today is the feast of St. Blaize and all the people go to church and get a special blessing for throat diseases. The church was full. I tried after church to get some sausage but there was none to be got. They will have some on Saturday but each person will get no more than half a pound. All meat is very scarce.

I feel so sorry for the children here as the shoes one sees are dreadful. These wooden shoes cannot be warm for they are all open at the back and <u>must</u> wear out their stockings. You see people with all kinds of things on their feet for warmth but all they say is: 'We must bear it all for the sake of the Fatherland'.

Their patience is really incredible. Even when they can't get butter and cheese etc. they only say: 'We must hold out'.

I wonder if in England the people help the government so. I can scarcely think that they have such patience. Or they have altered greatly since I left.

No news of the damage in England only the remark that the brave flyers have given England something to think of. There is news of a flying raid over Paris and a deal of damage done also over Salonica and many English soldiers killed.

Friday 4th February.

There is news of America but we have heard so much of that land. First over the **Lusitania,** which one reads in the reports and one wonders what it will lead to. Germany will not declare that her undersea boat war is illegal. Not even to suit America. She firmly believes that she is in the right and that God is with her and her alone. <u>America can try her bluff as long as she likes.</u>

I met yesterday Frau Voight and her sister Fraulein Shumaker. The husband of the former is in Ruhleben and was interviewed last February because they did not imprison them in India until February. Then Germany imprisoned also all her people who were born in India. Herr Voight was born in Calcutta. The brother of the two ladies, Herr Shumaker, is a painter and etcher and is doing a deal business in Ruhleben and is so busy that he cannot complete his orders. We had a long chat together and they seem very nice ladies.

Saturday 5th February.

No news in the paper today of America, but news of a Zeppelin being sunk at sea and all men lost. They also say that the Germans have sunk three large ships at the mouth of the Thames by undersea boats.

Steinoff writes me that our nut trees must be cut down and that all woollen woven goods (drawers and singlets etc.) are called up by the government. After they are supplied we get what is left for sale in the shops.

I feel a bit better and am able to sleep now for a few hours each night.

Alice Durselen says that she has had no word from England since she wrote of her mother's death. Letters seem to go all wrong and there is news that the American mails have ceased for five days.

Tuesday 8th February.

No news from the front but one thousand five hundred soldiers leave Hildesheim this week for France and Russia.

No news yet of America and most people think it will be settled all right. Germany does not want anymore enemies.

There is a great scarcity of food and stuffs that you cannot buy. If you go into a shop they dare not sell you six towels – only three. It is the same with sewing cotton etc. and of course all the fine stuffs that come from the outlands are not to be got and there is a great scarcity in cotton. Sugar is scarce and is now four pence a pound. Flour is also the same price and is not nice.

The Germans are very vexed at the treatment by the English captain of the people of the **Luftship L19** which was wrecked early this month. The captain of a fishing boat took nine men and promised to send help for the others. But bad weather came and all were drowned. Well, I think that he was right. If he had taken the lot (thirty in all) and his ship had only nine men and no arms or guns it would have been possible that they could have been overpowered by the Germans. That happened on the **Ancona** and of course the man must first protect himself. He saved what he could so he was not as heartless as they make out. One must remember what has happened in this war before one judges.

I feel better this past week and today we have tried again to get Arthur free for a week or so for there are many repairs to be done in Woltershausen and Steinoff and I do not understand them.

A young lady who came to visit me last Sunday says that her brother is a prisoner in England and his wife meets him every fourteen days. At Christmas she was invited to spend half a day with him and go to the concert given by the prisoners. I do think that it is hard here. If they can run the risk of spies in England why can't they here? Arthur is now sixteen months a prisoner and I have not been able to see him once.

Friday 11th February.

I have not heard from Arthur for over a fortnight and hope that he is not ill. I feel a little better myself, but only wish I could breathe better.

Things are very bad as regards food. Fat is really dreadful to get and one cannot manage on a quarter pound of butter or margarine a week. If only we had the nice peaceful days back again as now the finest present one can make you is a little flour or yeast. I received at Christmas three pounds of white flour and counted it my finest present. For even with money in your hand you cannot get more than three-and-a-half pounds per week.

My maid has just come in to tell me that she has no bread. I cannot get any for her. I have plenty of money but no more cards until Monday . She says that she will see her friend and borrow enough cards for one pound of bread and that she must divide it out.

We always cook vegetables for supper but the dark (rye) bread weighs very heavy when you buy it fresh. Three slices is the allowance for the day and the loaves are bigger than our two pound loaves at home. Three slices are half a pound and they only allow now six ounces per day. I tell my maid that she must put a mark for each day in the loaf when she gets it and then she must eat no more than her allowance.

Fresh meat is dreadfully scarce and most of the butchers are closed.

One of my enquarterings (soldiers) went on Thursday morning. He is such a nice fellow and an only child. His parents send him enough money, but though he had money he could not buy any butter or meat to pack up for himself. A servant girl spent over two hours searching the town to get him a quarter pound of butter and a little sausage. The poor fellow had only been gone a few hours to the front when a large parcel came from his mother. It had been delayed in the post. He has gone to France and had no desire to go there. He preferred Russia because their shooting is so good in France and so many fall there. I am so sorry for him. I wonder when the last one will go away. It will not be long before he follows his friend.

Saturday 12th February.

There is news of the sinking of a French ship, the Admiral something, with eight hundred men on board. She sank within two minutes and not one life was saved. There is great rejoicing here but we do not see any announcement from the French minister in Paris. It is dreadful to think of all those lives lost in two minutes.

Tuesday 15th February.

Winnie's birthday. I have sent Arthur a parcel for his birthday and hope that he gets it for the 18th.

No news of the French ship but they think it is the **Saffron** and not the Admiral something, but one does not know what to believe. These German names for the foreign ships are so strange to read.

We read that no more prisoners are to be taken alive and that all must be shot. I wonder if this is true. On the 28th a great sea battle is to take place, or commence, and all ships are to be sunk without warning – neutral or not.

I had good news today. The police sent me a notice that it would suit them if I only went once a week to announce instead of every day. <u>That's very nice of them.</u> One of the officers met me on the staircase one day last week and said that he got a shock to see me. I looked so very ill. He is a nice fellow and said: 'If you don't pick up, your good man will not know you when he returns'.

The next day another officer asked me if any special day would suit me to announce myself. I asked him if he had a new order for prisoners of war (civil) and he said: 'No, but we are going to make one for you'.

As a result a letter was sent to me yesterday and I went to thank them and arranged for Wednesday. Herr Rult remarked: 'That is six times a week less for you to mount these stairs and I am glad for your sake'.

They are very kind to me and are only doing their duty. But one does as a rule think the police awfully officious.

Friday 18th February.

This is Arthur's second birthday in Ruhleben, and a rotten place to celebrate it in. I hope that he gets his parcel, I sent him a pudding.

Yesterday I had a visit from Frau Voight and her sister Fraulein Schumacher with little Thea Voight – such a charming little girl. Frau V. is so angry about her man being imprisoned. She tells me that they lived in Bremen and on December 2nd a policeman came and said all Englanders must go out of the town in twenty-four hours and must get more inland. They had to close up their house and come here and live in a hotel.

They have relations in Hannover but were not allowed to go there. Her brother, who was naturalised in England and was in Ruhleben, had a flat locked up in Berlin so they asked for permission to go to live there. It was not allowed and of the places left open they chose Hildesheim. On February the 9th her husband was imprisoned and they have lived here ever since. I asked her how it was her husband was free until then and that mine went in November. She said her husband was in India, naturalised, and that they did not imprison the Germans in India until February the 3rd and then Germany did the same with the naturalised Indians here. Her husband was a trader in India but was educated at Rugby in England and has a great love for that land.

There is news of great unrest in Berlin but it is from a private source for nothing is in the papers. They say the people have demanded peace and bread and also that the same has happened in Hannover. That is too dreadful to believe and one wonders where it will all end.

We read in the papers that yesterday the fortress of Erzurum has been taken by the Russians from the Turks. We have noticed for a few days in the Russian reports that several forts had fallen but nothing was reported here. There is a very small account of the battle in our papers but reading the reports of France, Russia and England it seems a great victory.

There is also an account of the speeches of Prince Leopold von Bayern and I was surprised at his language. He spoke of his enemies as so: 'God damn the Englander and God give bad luck to all the French'.

I forget the <u>prayer</u> for the Russian but it is scarcely to be believed that an educated man, yet alone a Prince, will so far forget himself as to use such language. This war has much to answer for.

Wednesday 23rd February.

Heard from Alice Graeinghoff today and she sent me Lena's and Emily's letters about their mother's death. They have taken two weeks to come.

Food is very scarce here and the bread is awful to eat and potatoes are not to be got from the shops. You can get them from the Red Cross Society, but they are only sold in small quantities of five or ten pounds to each person. When you remember that there is only six ounces of bread per day to eat one must cook potatoes for dinner or suffer so. Of course many potatoes are required.

We got today a continental edition of the 'Daily Mail' and there is a very good article in it of the sinking of two German boats - we never heard of it here - The **Pommern** and **no. 126**. I wonder when it happened. There is also a very good article by a man who signs himself, 'an Englishman called Pecknsniff of the war'. I am sorry I cannot keep the paper.

They mention also the failure of three German banks and we have not heard of that at all.

I went today for my weekly visit to the police. It's the first time and I must say that it is most agreeable.

Friday 25th February.

The food shortage is getting very serious indeed and you can go all over town and not get any. And that is with money and tickets in your hand. A cabbage costs one shilling (for five persons) and sprouts are seven pence a pound. Potatoes are not to be got and many bakers are to be closed. Children come to your door and beg for a ticket to buy a little bread. Money they have but no bread cards or tickets.

They announce today that we are all to be allowed three-quarters-of-a-pound of potatoes a person per day and with the six ounces of bread it means hunger for so many things fail in the grocers and butchers. Fresh meat is at a discount and most shops are closed and you are not able to get more than half-a-pound of sausage at once.

I have been getting potatoes from the estate up to now but Steinoff tells me that there are to be no more. What is there is required for seeds.

It is wonderful how the people hold together for their Fatherland and are so economical.

Just fancy, it has been impossible to get a bit of bacon or an ounce of lard since December 1st and margarine at a quarter-of-a-pound per household a week and it is one shilling and eight pence per pound. Butter is sold ditto and most weeks it is not to be got and four days a week the people are without fat. It is forbidden to be used, to make it last longer, and in no house is baking allowed. If you buy flour to cook with, then you have none to make bread. It must be dreadful where there is a family for you cannot buy rice, extra flour, oatmeal etc. for money. I sometimes wonder how it will all end.

There has been trouble in Berlin, and even here, but most people are very patient with it all and only say: 'We must hold out until the end'.

Sunday 27th February.

Belle reads today of the Russian successes. They seem to be joining the English in Asia, but here they announce (from the Turkish reports) that it is a mere nothing.

Yesterday the flags were flying for the fall of a fort in Verdun and ten thousand French prisoners were taken. We hear of the dreadful 'trummel fire' being heard at Metz all day Thursday and Friday morning so we knew that there was a big battle in progress. God help those people who have relatives in that quarter. There are so many from here that have sons in Verdun. It is too dreadful to think of. We have no particulars up to now only the fall of one fort and the ten thousand prisoners.

Two more priests have gone to the front from here and that is two hundred and twenty-six from the diocese of Hildesheim. We have two from Alsace Lorraine here to help and they must announce to the police each day like I did.

Monday 28th February.

We hear today that America will not allow that Germany does sink all neutral ships and has placed impossible conditions in the way.

People are beginning to say now that they dread after the war for so much money will be wanted for widows and orphans and that the very high taxes are sure to be higher still. We are anxiously awaiting the new taxation.

The newspapers are trying to <u>buck</u> up the people by saying that we must take it as a duty to the Fatherland. I think of how much worse it would be for us if the enemy came all through the land and did as they did in East Prussia and destroy all our goods and premises.

I am so sorry for the poor people, they must be so hungry.

I had a letter from Arthur yesterday and he has hopes of coming for a couple of weeks leave. I am afraid to hope any more.

Steinoff has written for him and the 'mayor' of the village has stamped and signed it for him and we are anxiously awaiting the result.

I went to the Wiener Hof Hotel today to have a cup of tea with Frau Voight. It was like going home and all were so glad to see me. I suppose that after ten months in residence there they look upon me as an old guest.

Wednesday 1st March.

There are new rules on the bread cards and people are beginning to get uneasy about food. So many shops are closed and it is dreadful to get potatoes. Even wealthy people are asking you to let them have twenty pounds of your store and they will return it later on. Even with money in their pockets the people are really hungry.

My enquarterings told my maid that they were satisfied after their supper here every week. They come here once a week to supper, though I pay for their lodging and coffee elsewhere, and it was the only time each week that they left feeling full. They always ask for bread cards so they can buy extra bread and I have none to spare.

Real food is scarce and very dear. When a person has bought three-and-a-half pounds of bread a week they have no cards for flour. So it is impossible to make a pancake or thicken the soup. Vegetables are at a discount and sprouts are seven pence per pound, a cabbage is one shilling, swedes two pence per pound, and so on. Dried peas and beans are very scarce and dear at five pence and sixpence per pound. Just try how far one pound of those will go. The worst are the potatoes and they are a shilling a score, but you cannot get them. I guarantee that if you went in every shop in this town this morning you would not get a pound.

They are only available through the Red Cross Society for the poorest people and are sold on cards at five pounds for each person. You have to live on five pounds of spuds, three-and-a-half pounds of bread and whatever else you can afford to buy at an extraordinary price. Meat is two shillings a pound, and butter is two shillings and eight pence to be got only in quarter pounds. Rice, lentils, flour and cornflower are not to be got and milk is very scarce with one pint being allowed for three people unless you have a doctor's note for more on account of sickness.

Yet the people hold together wonderfully and say we must help the Fatherland. I often wonder where it would end were it in England.

The small white breads are a halfpenny each and ten make up a pound. White bread is now five pence per pound and the dark bread is so awful to eat that sometimes I save bread cards and buy one pound of flour that costs four pence and I must give one-and-a-quarter pounds of bread cards for that. The system is really marvellous and there is no possibility of dodging.

Today we read a Russian report to the effect that they have completely demoralised Persia and that the Turks have fled from them. There is no question about the report so it must be true though no provenance was given to it in the paper. Also the French report that they got back the west side of the lost fortress before Verdun. There are no remarks on that. I fancy that it must be true.

How long is this war going to last I wonder?

Thursday 2nd March.

The war news from here is scarce but according to the French reports the Germans are surrounded in the fort they took on Friday last. One cannot believe it. I daresay that the French papers are like all the others and tell lies to suit themselves. No news from Russia at all, but the people hear that the war will last another year. I wonder if the Russian report is true and that the Turks and Persians are completely routed.

Hermenia came today and she says that they have not heard anything of the letter that went to Ruhleben. I am beginning to lose what bit of hope I had. And that was not much.

Lots in the paper about the new war loan (the 4th) and they beg of the people to put every shilling in it as it is their solemn duty. Every school child must take its savings and put it in, but people are so poor and food is so dear. One never sees the big fat soldiers that we had at first and now everyone is so thin. I never was so thin in my life before and many say the same for the food is not nutritious and the scarcity of fat is telling on all - rich and poor - young and old.

Tuesday 7th March.

Today I had a visit from Herr Vieweg. He is let out of Ruhleben for leave for an indefinite time. He brought me news of Arthur and we had a long chat together. He has improved his English very much in his time in Ruhleben. He tells me that they have classes amongst themselves and go to school just like boys. He has studied English and reads and writes it very well. So you see that even in the late thirties it is possible to commence studies again. It's never too late to learn. This is the gentleman who called on me twelve months ago having leave to visit his doctor. He brought me some of the literature they published in Ruhleben and the small books are very funny. They are published every two weeks and cost two pence. I do hope that Arthur is collecting them.

I heard also that England is exchanging three German prisoners for every Englishman and that three hundred and twenty-five English leave Ruhleben this week and that one thousand Germans come back to Germany. This is not in the papers. All are to be over forty-five-years-old this year and as Arthur is forty-five this year we hope for his release. Arthur is very busy and often works till twelve o'clock at night. We are hoping to hear from him soon.

In the papers it states that the Germans are just before Verdun. The French report says they have been driven back again. One cannot believe the papers at all.

Wednesday 8th March.

Had a letter from Arthur and he thinks that he will get a few days leave at the end of this month. He says that he has met the son of Herr Richstoffen (from Blackpool) in

Ruhleben. He says that food is more a trouble for us than them.

One spends all their time in wondering what to cook with the material at hand and all is so adulterated. Permission is given to the people to "fake" their products to make them go further and receipts are given on how to boil butter with meal etc. to make it go further. <u>Life is one long dodge.</u> How is it, I want to know, that England can send dripping and butter from Denmark to Ruhleben and that Germany cannot get it for her markets? It's very funny to me.

Friday 10th March.

I received a letter yesterday from dad over America enclosing one from Kit written on the 31st December and one from James which was nearly a year old. They were such a pleasure to me.

I also had a visit from Frau Voight whilst she was here. Herr Vieweg came with his wife so we were a party. Mrs. Voight and I had our husbands in Ruhleben and Miss Shumaker has her brother there too. We told Mrs. Vieweg that she was a lucky woman to be having her husband to take her out to tea.

I do hope that Arthur comes through. Yet I want to be a little better before he comes.

Monday 13th March.

Had a disappointment today for I hear that Arthur has been refused his fourteen days release. I shall never again build up hope on him coming free until peace is declared.

The shortage of food is awful and so many shops are closed that it is pitiful to see. I sent my maid out for eight articles and she returned with two. The others were not to be had at all.

Friday 17th March.

St. Patrick's Day and a very beautiful spring day here.

We hear of the resignation of Admiral von Tirpitz and everyone here is astonished.

We hear that there is trouble in the town about bread and meat and that one must be thankful for small mercies in these times.

We have had a new consignment of wounded soldiers. They parked furniture vans here and laid beds on the floors of the vans. This was to make the men more comfortable. I saw seven men, all under thirty-years-old, and each man had lost his right leg. It was awful to see.

I have been busy today making soft soap as one has to try at all trades. Soft soap is one shilling and two pence per pound and is awful stuff. Scouring soap is two shillings and two pence so it is all very expensive. If my receipts turn out well I will have ten pounds in weight for five shillings and sixpence. That's a saving. We only clean the floors now once a week where before it was three times.

I have been strongly advised this week to auction the estate. I do not know which way to turn. Yet the advice, at present, looks very sound. If only I could get independent advice. I feel bound hand and foot here in a strange land.

Monday 20th March.

I have been to have a cup of tea with Mrs. Voight in the Wiener Hof and she tells me that she has heard that Herr Vieweg has been let free from Ruhleben because they are going to call him up for the military. If that is true I am thankful that they have not let Arthur free for he is better in Ruhleben than in the front.

No war news of any note only contradictions. The French say that they have not lost any places. The Germans say that they have got some. One does not know the truth. The Berlin papers say now that the resignation of Admiral Tirpitz is in consequence of a difference of opinion and that it had to be kept secret for some time. That sounds funny when one remembers the Kaiser wrote of regret for his ill health.

We are to have meat cards next month at so much meat a week. We don't know how much.

There has been a difference of opinion in the parliament and the Socialist has been giving a bit of his mind. A visitor here tells me that in Berlin the Social Democrat women stormed the house of their leader for giving his word that the Socialists should go in the war. At the beginning of the war the Socialists were all for the nation. Now they say that they are not being treated as they should be at the promises of 'one party only' and they are angry.

Even in Warsaw there is trouble and the Poles say that the Germans are not keeping their word of last November and are angry about it.

This war loan is finished today and they have canvassed every school. Every scholar has taken five shillings and upwards to his teacher. In one school twenty six thousand shillings have been collected. That is here in Hildesheim, we have seventeen schools, so that will help the war loan.

The Bishop of Metz has written to his churches that all their monies must be invested from the church funds into the war loan so it is sure to be a success. I wonder if we will have a 5th war loan in another four months.

We are having lovely spring weather and for the last week it has been so warm. The sun is so strong that we had no need for any fires in the middle of the day. On St. Patrick's Day we had no fires (only in the kitchen) until five o'clock in the evening.

Bread is so scarce and the bakers are often sold out at ten o'clock in the morning and many people have made a row at the town hall. One man went with card and money and would not leave without bread so they had to telephone to all the bakers. A woman with her six children said awful things so it all looks pretty serious.

Friday 24th March.

Got a letter from Willie today and also a photo of little Joan – she is a bonnie little girl – and I long to see her. Willie says all are well and that the news from Canada is good. That's a blessing.

I have not heard from Arthur for over two weeks and I expect that he is as disappointed as me about his leave.

Meat is very scarce and has gone up dreadfully in price and many days you can get none. Flour is not to be had at any price so you can use none for cooking. Bread we get at the bakers and it is awful stuff and so sour and the white bread is so dark and full of potatoes.

The war loan has reached ten million marks or shillings so there is still plenty of money still.

Sunday 26th March.

I have been today to hear a young priest celebrate his first Mass. It was a very elaborate but touching ceremony.

On the feast of St. Joseph three young priests were ordained and today they all celebrate their first high mass. One of them celebrates in the Dom (cathedral) for he and his parents are members of that congregation and the others celebrate theirs in their respective churches where they were brought up – one in Hildesheim and one in a village nearby.

At the beginning of the war there were nine young men in the seminary or church where they are educated for the priesthood. Those who were only in their minor orders had to go to the war, but those who had advanced were allowed to complete their studies and be ordained before they went away. Four went to the front in the first month of the war. Three are dead and one is wounded. He has lost a leg but is to be ordained for a cloister and he can become a monk. The three who were ordained last Saturday go to the front in a week or so. Then there is one left and when he is ordained the place will be empty and the seminary must close until there are more boys advanced enough in their schools to join the priesthood. It's very sad. Even the professors (priests) go away every so often to the front and we expect every week that the regent (the head of the seminary) will have to go for he is already called up. There are no young priests left and all around here those remaining are in their fifties and over.

I asked what they made of the priests in the military and they said that they are made sergeants and are given watch duty. It seemed very sad to think that this young man saying his first mass must go away soon. I felt so sorry for his parents and grandparents. What is not sad in these times? I feel sorry even for myself but how about the poor people?

Every week food is getting dearer and scarcer. Cocoa is now ten shillings a pound, coffee four shillings, tea six shillings, soap two shillings and two pence, meat and sausage two shillings and four pence and three shillings a pound and not to be got at all, sugar is only sold in half pounds and butter in a quarter. Fat of any description cannot be had. We hear that lard is to be sold for three days next week in one place at six shillings a pound. They can keep it at that price.

We hear today that Russia has publicly sold her German subjects' belongings so perhaps it will come here. One man said last week that if the war lasts much longer he is afraid that we shall have serious trouble over the food. There is a very bitter feeling against England again.

We hear of no more progress in Verdun. If only one could see the beginning of peace. It sometimes seems so far off and the anxiety of these days tells on one. The poor soldiers – I feel so much for them. Now we understand what a delightful time we lived in - in the days of peace. How small those little differences seem now – politics, education, income tax, free trade etc. in the face of this dreadful war.

We are now told that we must not have visitors and give them coffee or tea. Also we must not buy much material for our clothes so that there will be enough for all. No one can make these new wide skirts as it takes too much stuff. There is to be a new post tax next month and all is to be double price. The people are grumbling at that and we must not send Easter parcels to the field as luxuries are not required for the soldiers. We must consider the post which is very much understaffed and is closed for four hours in the middle of the day. In fact wherever you look it is serious.

It is now a month since the attack on Verdun commenced and we do not hear of its fall, though it is expected every day.

We read here that it is much worse in England for everything is scarce and the people are quarrelling amongst themselves very much.

A lady called to see me last week and a sister of hers is a nurse in a lazarett and she says that the French prisoners are very willing to help in the work and are very polite. The Russian will do what you tell him and is very obedient. But the Englishman is neither polite nor obedient and is very lazy. He will refuse to do even a simple job and he is the most unsatisfactory prisoner they have. Now, that is the second time I have heard the same complaint from two different lazaretts and I feel ashamed of the Englishmen. Such unthankfulness is dreadful to the people who nurse and attend them. Even if it is not as good as home it is better than nothing and one must be thankful for small mercies in these times of war.

Friday 31st March.

No war news of any note but a lot in the papers about the conference in Paris and that England has threatened to break the neutrality of Holland.

A lot of soldiers left here very hurriedly this week at only two hours notice. Many left home in the morning just to drill and never returned to say goodbye. They left the barracks straight away. They must have received urgent summons.

We read that Mrs. Asquith has been fined one thousand pounds for playing tennis with the prisoners (German). I don't believe it.

We have had such a lot of fliers here this past two days – eight or nine in the air at once. They land and start off on a high meadow near the river. I have been to see them and it is very interesting.

Saturday 1st April.

Got a letter from Arthur today and he says that Ettie has written to him as regards Winnie at school. She is now fourteen but I wish her to have another year study and then we will decide what to do with her.

It is not true about Mrs. Asquith (we read in a neutral paper – Swiss) and that 'The Globe' had to pay her one thousand pounds for slander. So now the boot is on the other foot.

Many men are going away today and my servant's young man has been called. He has ten days leave and it is his first for eight months. He had only been here for four days when he found out that he must return. He left here at six o'clock and arrived at eleven o'clock at night in Halle. He was re-clothed and on the train for Russia at half-past two in the morning and not a minute of sleep. It was sharp work.

Prices are rising very much and we expect double post rates this week with letters costing two pence and post-cards a penny and so on. Everything is to be at double price.

Tuesday 4th April.

There is great excitement this last three days about Holland. It is reported that England has made her mobilise and that the Germans have had to send many men to the Dutch frontier. I cannot believe it but the men were sent off in a great hurry.

They announce also that Asquith has been received by the Pope and that the Italians have once more turned around. They thought here that Italy was tired of England.

Thursday 6th April.

A big change in the weather and last night we had a violent thunderstorm and all the nice cherry and apricot blossom has been destroyed.

No special war news and there is nothing definite in the papers about Holland. Germany is quite prepared for whatever happens.

There are new rules about eating and every restaurant or hotel has to close two days a week and nothing to eat must be sold. There are two days without fresh meat and another two days nothing is to be cooked with fat. That is no fried or roasted, only boiled. Sunday is the only day you can have a real meal (dinner).

One day last week a man came here to see all the food you have in the house and you do not know that they are coming. They simply come in and ask to see your goods for you are not allowed more than a certain quantity in store or stock.

It is quite a trial about bread and I know people of money who are sometimes a whole day without bread and must eat potatoes and salt for breakfast and also for supper (tea time we do not have here) and many people are three and four days together without butter. If that is the case where people have money, what about those who have none? My servant is often two days without bread for she is a big hungry girl and eats her seven days bread up in five days. When you have no bread cards you can get no bread. Everything is scarce and dear. There is not one thing that is not dear and bread and butter are a <u>great</u> luxury. You cannot give them to a visitor for money will not buy them. Even the newspapers have risen in price because paper is so dear.

Everyone expects that something is going to happen in the next few weeks and they are looking to the Belgium and Dutch frontier for it to happen.

Such a lot of fliers have been here this week with eight or ten in the air at once.

Saturday 8th April.

The Chancellor's speech seems to have upset things. The people say now that there is no likelihood of peace for some time. There is trouble with the Social Democrat leader but the papers are forbidden to print the speeches.

We hear from a private source of great trouble in Berlin and also in several small towns that smallpox has broken out. Thirty-six cases in one town but it is not in the papers. People have come here to visit to be out of danger. We had a visitor here from Göttingen and she tells us that we are well off here. In Göttingen they have had only three ounces of butter per person per week for a long time and many other things are not to be had. She took goods back with her from here but not butter as that is impossible to be got.

I often see the children going to the good Sisters of Charity for their dinner. It's a great blessing that we have them in Hildesheim. The children get their cards in the schools and so many of the poor go to the convent for dinner. How the Sisters must work for they feed about eight hundred a day. Also the poor people can take their cards and a dish and then take enough home for the family dinner instead of eating it there. It is really pitiful to see the old men and women with a small enamel bucket with a lid going to get their hot pot for a penny a pint. There is more water put in it when they get home and the family is fed. The Sisters do a great charity.

It is sad to see the feet of the children with their slippers made from sacking. They have five or six old stocking feet sewn together, one over the other. Others have wooden soles on old shoes that are falling to pieces. Worst of all are the little ones going to school in felt slippers in the pouring rain. It makes me quite ill to see them and knowing that there is no fire or food at the back of it all, and no end in view. All say that we must hold out till the end.

We hear that Asquith returned to England after his Rome trip to find all his party against him. I don't believe it at all.

I had a letter from Johanna Pulmann today and she says that she has seen Arthur for a minute. He told her that I was to ask permission to visit him for now they are allowed to see their nearest relation. I have applied for permission and it will take fourteen days to get an answer. I do not have any hopes of being allowed to travel.

Tuesday 11th April.

Got a letter from Arthur saying that he would not sell the estate until he was able to look after it himself. I only hope that it is not too late. In Ruhleben one cannot write all one has to say.

There seems to be a depression at present. Certainly one looks a deal differently on life when one is never full of food. What you do buy is all imitation or an adulteration – 'ersatz' they call it here.

I am having a deal of trouble with my stomach for this last three months and hope that it does not result in another ulceration. But it seems like it. I have been having medical treatment for three months for it.

I hear through a friend from Ruhleben that Arthur is anxious for me to go to England. <u>That is not to be thought of</u>. Firstly I will not cross the water in this sharper undersea boat war and secondly I cannot go into a neutral land for the bank will not send me any money out of this land. They are forbidden to do so and you are not allowed to cross the frontier with anything of value on you and no gold at all. Even your wedding ring is taken from you and held until after the war.

I got good news today in a letter from Arthur in which he says I can visit him. I have sent up for permission and one hour is allowed. So, very likely, it is to be soon after Easter. That is something to look forward to.

This morning a gentleman came to see me, he is retiring on a pension from the saving bank, and he would like to rent Woltershausen. I hope that he takes it since Arthur does not think of selling it.

No war news of any note but there is news of a sharper blockade of Germany by England. It does not make the people here friendlier.

Got a letter from Willie today with Christmas greetings and it was posted on December 19th.

I have been working on the garden a little and planting various small things – parsley, onions, carrots and beans – for I do believe that this war will last at least one more year and it's best to be on the safe side. One did not know before the war how thankful to be for 'our daily bread'. We know it now and every bit of land is being cultivated. Beans, potatoes, cabbage and carrots flourish in the front gardens and are more taken care of than flowers. We were living in too much luxury (sometimes I forget the English words).

I am very busy at the moment spring cleaning.

There is a lot of sickness here including diphtheria and smallpox. There is also typhoid. One cannot wonder for all are underfed, rich and poor alike, as the food one gets is so scarce and poor.

I had news today that upset me. A friend has written that he gets the 'Times' of London and that he reads in it a famous lie that there has been an attack by the mob on Ruhleben. It was because the people are so angry that the Englander gets better food out of England than they get here. I do not believe it at all. It is very likely there has been unpleasantness. But as regards an attack I do not believe. The German people are too under the law of militarism for that. They have not the impudence of the Englishman.

Saturday 15th April.

We read today from an island paper that over one thousand and one hundred people were killed by the last raid of April 1st to 4th of the Zeppelins over England. It's too dreadful for words. I am always upset when I hear of their trips and one of these was over Leeds. I had such uneasiness about Winnie but by the account in the papers no damage was done there.

I hope that in a few days to get leave to visit Arthur but I shall not build upon it. I have had too many disappointments.

They are preparing here for the war to last at least twelve months longer and all food supplies are now so scarce. I heard on Wednesday that an attempt had been made on Ruhleben by the people of Berlin. That was upsetting news but how true one cannot say as there is such a strict censure of all papers here.

The news of the Turks does not seem bright for them and the Russians have won a little by Riga. Verdun is the same as last week but the Germans report progress by the river Iser in Flanders.

We hear of great unrest in England about the conscription and they say here that the masses will not join to save their country. Also there has been a deal of bloodshed in Ireland. Why cannot people let all their differences be on one side until this war is at an end?

Tuesday 18th April.

Today we expect the sharper blockade of England and an answer to the American note.

Things cannot go much worse in the food line for the scarcity and the badness of the eatables is not at an end. All animals are now confiscated by the government as so much food is not to be got. All is scarce and lots of articles are entirely run out. It is providence that we have been able to get food from Romania. There seems to be a settled depression on all the folk.

I have decided not to let the house in Woltershausen. The garden is of more use to me as you cannot buy the food.

I am anxiously awaiting the result of my petition to visit Arthur but I shall not build up on it until it is really granted.

We hear today that the food stuffs bought from Romania have cost so much money that all the food baked from there (breadstuffs) will be three times the price. For example a loaf costs nine-and-a- half pence (black bread) and from this meal from Romania it will cost two shillings and two pence so it will be very dear stuff.

All cakes were forbidden to be baked for the confirmations or for Easter and no one dare bake at home.

We have just heard a good joke. It says in the German 'Punch' that we have two days without meat, and two days without fat, so to save the clothes stuffs we are to have two days a week without clothes. It is true that all materials are very scarce and very dear.

We are very quiet at Wörth Strasse and spend a few hours a day receiving visitors or paying calls. Then I must cook. This girl cannot yet cook to please me, or rather my stomach. We live a very regular life and half past nine each night sees us in bed.

A lady here tells me that her husband, who is in Ruhleben, has written to say that Herr Dröege is anxious to get his wife to England. Well, I shall not go. Firstly I should be anxious about him and secondly I should be afraid to cross the water with their underwater boat war. It is no use to think of it at all.

Saturday 22nd April.

Read today that the Russians have landed in Marseilles (France) at Verdun and that a German General has died in Turkey of typhoid. Also that the Russians have got two more places on the sea coast by the Black Sea.

I have no news yet of my proposed visit.

The butcher tells me that there will be no meat for three weeks as the government has given orders for no slaughtering for twenty-one days. Mutton is now three shillings a pound, veal three shillings and two pence and fat of all kinds put together and rendered is four shillings a pound. Soft soap is not to be got and we are to have soap cards and each household is to get one pound a month for cleaning and a quarter-of-a-pound per month for toilet.

White dresses are forbidden to be worn and the children must be allowed to run about bare foot to save the shoe leather for winter. I am so glad that I do not have a family.

24th April Easter Monday.

Great excitement about America but I do not think that it will come to anything. We have had excitement from these people many times and it has always blown over. I wonder what they can do even if they do come into the war.

Today is lovely weather and just like mid summer and Uncle George Steffen called on me and is here on a visit for a few days. He talked of Woltershausen and of the very happy days that we had spent there. He is in military service but having had an operation three years ago here he is given garrison duty and looks very well.

There is still no news of my Berlin visit.

Friday 28th April.

I have got permission to travel to Woltershausen next week.

No news of America but there is great unrest about the answer.

We read of the arrest of Rodger Casement. It's a funny business and one does not know what to believe of the various tales, but it seems to be very serious. I think it is a disgrace of Ireland and especially during these times when there is so much suffering. Here the people are so united and put up with much worse than ever an English or Irish person would dream of.

All the meat shops have been closed this week. Seven days and not able to buy one ounce of meat and we do not know if we can get any in the morning. It is said that every person will be allowed one quarter-of-a- pound of meat per week, two ounces of butter or margarine, three-and-a-half pounds of bread and five pounds of potatoes. That is to be our allowance and we have cards for it. Whether you can get it is another question. You can go in half the shops in town and get none of the above articles for money or cards.

I think it is utterly impossible for us to last three months longer if all transactions are cut off from America. We do not hear of any of those food stuffs being here from Romania.

We hear this week that Russians have landed for the second time in France. It is said that they came over Norway as workers and were sent to England, fitted out as soldiers, then shipped to France - but this is only paper talk.

Saturday 29th April.

News tonight of the surrender of Kut-Al-Amara and thirteen thousand Englishmen have been made prisoners. I am sorry for General Townsend and am sure that they held out for as long as possible.

There is news of the Irish rebellion and they say that Dublin is in the hands of the Fenians and all telephone communications are cut off. That has been a dreadful business throughout and I feel thoroughly ashamed of Ireland.

Monday 1st May.

I travelled today to Woltershausen to plant a few things there and to arrange about the garden. It was a glorious day but it was sad to see the place so neglected.

We commenced the new time today and all the clocks were put on one hour at midnight so all the pubs close at eleven o'clock instead of twelve o'clock to allow the people to get earlier to bed. One did not remark the difference as it is so light in the morning. In the land they have not altered their time for they say that they must work by the sun and it is too hot at noon. Also the cattle must not be fed one hour later as it will make a difference in the amount of milk produced.

They had the impudence to ask me if I would pay the rent of the electricity for the house as if we were living in it. I told them: 'No, it was not my fault that we were no longer living there and burning the light'.

Also I get no interest on my money.

I bought some 'quassa' chips today to boil and use as soap for washing. They have none in the village at all and it's a bad thing for them. We boil the chips in water, it smells like ammonia, and then we wash in it. It makes quite a lather and using soda is more complicated.

They announce a 'compelled' war loan where every man (single) who earns over sixteen shillings a week has not to be paid the difference and his employer has to give him the sixteen shillings and pay the remainder into a savings bank. Through this bank he must invest all his extra money in the new 'forced' war loan and it is to commence in June. The people do not like it but say 'we must'. I believe that there has been trouble in the industries about it.

We hear that all troops are being taken from Verdun and sent to Ypres and there is to be a great battle there and then Ypres is to fall and then Calais. How long is this dreadful time still to last?

I got some eggs yesterday and they were four for a shilling. Steinoff tells me that a suckling pig of ten pounds weight costs forty-five to fifty shillings.

Saturday 6th May.

We are awaiting the answer to the German note sent to America and there seems to be great anxiety about it now.

We read of the failure of the compelled war loan as the men in the industries will not have it.

We have not so many soldiers here now and it's a good thing for food is so scarce and there is a great deal of suffering. We get a quarter of butter, a quarter of meat, seven pounds of bread and ten pounds of potatoes for fourteen days. That is all there is allowed. You must fill up with jams, macaroni or whatever you have or can buy.

We are having perfect weather with every good prospect for the crops. Many people say that we can hold out for two more years at the present state of affairs as regards food but not as regards men.

The soldiers get fewer and fewer and many houses are without enquarterings now and one remarks that in the streets there are not many uniforms.

They say today that Sweden has written to England and Russia and that it looks like war. They are angry with Russia but one gets so many of these shocks that one gets used to them. I myself think that the American note will end like it did last June and July.

I found out last week that I had lost or had stolen three coats (two silk and one cloth), a pair of trousers and a black satin underskirt. I do not know who to blame so I have called in the police.

Friday 12th May.

The note from America has arrived and the people here are angry at the way it was received in America. Wilson has a nice name at present.

Things are no better here and there is no news of my visit to Berlin.

I had a letter from Arthur asking for some of his underclothes and I find that they have also been stolen which is rather disagreeable as everything is so scarce.

Monday 15th May.

The talk of the people and the papers is all about food. It is awfully scarce and every day we are having trouble. There was a revolution in Brunswick last week but there was nothing in the papers though it is freely talked of amongst the people here.

The bakers are sold out at eight o'clock and of course the butcher is only opened for a few hours each Saturday morning.

The butter is mostly brought by women from the various dairies in the land and sold to the houses. Now the people waylay these butter women in the streets and forcibly take the butter away and throw in their baskets the money and cards. It's the same with the bakers. The boys dare not go out to deliver bread as the people waylay them. Everyone must go to the shops themselves and push in with the crowd. It is really the survival of the fittest. If you cannot go in the crowd and fight for your bit you get nothing. We seem to have gone back to the time of the savage now it comes to famine. I could write pages and pages about the food question.

I am keeping well at present but Belle has been four days in the Krankenhaus as she had to have her teeth out and chloroform was necessary. She is now at home again and getting better.

There is terrible lot of sickness here at present and I suppose it comes from the nerves and the poor food. I know lots of people who have had no butter for two or three weeks and often it is impossible to get bread and meat (a quarter pound). It is not allowed to sell cans of meat or sausage.

No news from Verdun but I have an old London Times of last year and the news is very different from what we heard. I wonder which land lies.

Friday 19th May.

It's no use me writing the war news for what I read one day is contradicted or no notice given to it the next day. Then I know it is not to be believed. In future I shall keep to my own private affairs and how the war affects me.

At present I am well but begin to feel my disappointments about my visit to Arthur for it is now seven weeks since they received visitors. Though I wrote up at once for permission to visit him I have not even received a line to say that my request is being considered. We are having lovely spring weather and I work in the garden and keep generally busy.

There is no news of the thief of my clothes.

The news from America is reported very favourably in the papers with no fear of war.

We read that they are going to have the new time in England and all clocks are put back one hour. It acts very well here and after the first day we did not notice it at all as we all go to bed at ten o'clock. We have never had a light on in our house for two weeks and the only difference is that we feel it cold in the mornings until about nine o'clock.

We are to have a general soup kitchen in all towns after this month and everyone has to give up all he has in his store room in the meat line – ham, bacon, sausage and meat in tins or jars. Every day there will come along a soup wagon and we are to get a quantity of soup for two pence halfpenny and everyone has to eat the same. All is to be cooked together, meat, cabbage, potatoes etc and sold as a thin 'hotpot'. It is the same food as the soldier gets.

From today no baker dare sell more than two pounds of bread at a time to one person. It is because the people have been getting more than their share early in the week and then when their cards are done at the weekend they get angry because they cannot get any more bread. Now they are to be prevented from using it all up early. Rice, sago, tapioca and macaroni are not to be had so there is nothing to fill up with. The butcher gets his meat early on the Saturday morning each week and we all get our quarter pound per person per week. Yet the people will meet you and say: 'We have enough to live on. Before the war we ate too much'.

Perhaps so and I do not think I have as large an appetite. But a quarter pound of butter in two weeks is too little for me. We also have a quarter pound of meat and bread at three-and-a-half pounds for seven days. I have these and the ten pounds of potatoes, but they do not fill me.

Lots of butchers sell fish on certain days. The town eating offices (all the food supply comes through one set of offices) say we can get fish, say twice a week. Codfish is available on those days and certain people eat cheaper fish as codfish is eight pence per pound and fluke costs ten pence per pound. The cheaper ones are very small fish and for two pounds of cod you get three or four of the small fish. With fluke you get five for a pound so they are not very advantageous.

Coffee is very scarce and dare not be sold without half coffee and half adulterations of a certain coffee meal. Cocoa is not to be had. Tea is eight pence a pound and rotten at that. It is a fact no one has much to cook these days - only potatoes.

I had a line from Alice Graeinghoff (Durselen) and she says that she has been at Baden-Baden to take the baths and she wonders how she will find it at home. She had enough to eat in the bath's pension. Her daughter had said that they had no coffee or butter for over two weeks and could Alice bring some home for them. But you get nothing without cards and you must be a householder to get them and not a guest at a pension. The manageress is so good that not a thing can be got without cards so you only get your portions.

What does surprise me are the people. No grumbling is to be heard and you hear no one speak of losing. One day last week this remark was made to me: 'In 1866 the

Austrians had to, and in 1871 the French. Now it is our turn. We are all human beings and what they had to do, we can do. Only we will not be beaten as they were. We shall win by our holding out'.

I often wonder if the people are of the same mind in England. If this is the result of militarism then there is certainly a deal to be said in its favour. The obedience amongst so many people is to be admired.

I think so very often about all the men at home and if this new conscription will affect any of them. According to James' letter he is not accepted because of his eyes and George is too far out in the land (Canada) I should think. But Willie, John, Robert etc. I often wonder about.

Arthur does not say that he has any letters lately from home and that always makes me uneasy.

Here we are having lovely weather and I wonder so often of George and Kittie, so far out in the country in British Columbia. Spring is so very beautiful when one is in the very centre of nature as they are. I wonder if I shall ever see their homes and Kittie's little one. I think so often of them all.

Monday 29th May.

Got a letter from Arthur yesterday and he says that he has to give my name and address. He thinks I shall get permission to visit him in a few days. Perhaps the wish is father to the thought. I have no hopes now for it is nine weeks since I wrote.

A lady who wrote later than I did has had her permission for over a week. I often wonder if it has anything to do with our strictness and that the family were such staunch Hanoverians. However, the lady wishes to travel with me to Berlin for company and then both go to Ruhleben together. She says she will go to the police here this week and ask them to make enquiries as to why I haven't received permission to visit my husband. At least we shall know why. That is some satisfaction.

I have been so distressed this week about the conscription in England. If only I could get news from home and hear about the men of the family. I am tired of praying for them all as there seems to be no answer to my prayers.

Arthur writes me that he has had a short letter from Winnie, but she writes of nothing but her own health. It's a pleasure to know all is well and we are keeping pretty well here and are having a few days wet weather.

There is a note in the paper that no more malt etc. is to be used for beer and that we can do without it. It is only a luxury, so my next delivery of bottles must be half <u>small beer</u> as we call it in England or herb beer. Also there are to be two days a week in the pubs and hotels when no beer is sold. So now we are six days without meat (you eat your quarter pound on a Sunday), two days without beer, and butter you only get at home and that's a quarter pound in fourteen days.

The new daylight bill is now quite ordinary to us and we very soon got used to it and it is a great saving. It seems very strange to be at the door in the evening and see the streets quite empty at ten o'clock and then think that it is really only nine o'clock. Hildesheim is a garrison town and the soldiers must be in by nine o'clock, so by ten o'clock the streets are quite empty. We have no theatres open as they are all lazaretts. There are no men to sit in the pubs as they are all soldiers.

We hear of great defeats in Italy. The poor Italian soldiers seem to be having a dreadful time. In France the Germans and French seem to be suffering dreadfully. The poor men, it seems too awful to think about. When will this war come to an end? One wonders how they live through the awful days let alone the fighting. Now the people here are quite delighted when they hear that one of their relatives is a prisoner: 'Thank God; he will come back to us after the war'.

It is the universal expression and every paper is full of it. I think it is to take our attention off the food question and also off the war places.

One can read from the French reports that there has been fighting by Verdun and one day it is in the French favour and the next in the German.

We have a notice that all nickel money is now to be called up and another five million marks in iron money is to be put into circulation. The nickel is for bullets. We have had a quantity of iron money for sometime but now all nickel is to go.

Another notice says that we have to take our bread book and we shall be allowed to buy for two pence halfpenny each one egg per person, per week, from the town offices. Each day a district will be attended to so I get three eggs per week, i.e. Belle, the servant girl and I. The farmers, being so short of meat (they dare not kill anything), are eating the eggs themselves and preserving them for winter so they are very scarce. They are three for a shilling and only a few to be had. People go to the country every Sunday to buy what they can and go from house to house like pedlars. They all end up with the cry: 'We must hold out. At this rate of living we can last two years at least'.

I don't think I can.

I went to the Doctor last week (I have been going for over a year) and he ordered me to take the baths again in Salzdetfurth. He said it was no use him giving me a note to the magistrate for more milk and butter for he had written for it for another invalid and the reply was: 'We cannot give what we have not got'.

<u>Very true.</u>

Sunday 4th June.

Lots of war news these last few days. On Friday 2nd we flagged for the great sea battle and on May 31st we celebrated the great battle in Italy where the Austrians took two of the principal forts off the Italians.

Many German soldiers in the Austrian uniform have left here this week and it is reported that a German General (Mackenson) has taken the forts. The Austrians are no good as soldiers and soon want to give up. The Germans must always be behind them and push them along.

The sea battle was a great day here and they reported that the whole of the English war fleet was present and also the whole of the German. The English list of lost ships is twelve certain and many reported missing. The German loss is four ships and three missing. If all we hear is true then England has had a great whacking. They report that the war ship **Westfalen** has sunk six English ships alone. Altogether it has been a great victory and all papers up to now (neutral etc.) remark that it is the greatest battle in history, and that Trafalgar was a fool to it. We read no notices from England. All we read is that the English Admiral in London says: 'We have lost the ships **Queen Mary, Invincible, Indefatigable, Defence, Blanche, Black Prince, Turbulent, Tipperary, Fortune, Sparrowhawk** and **Ardent**. Other ships are still missing'.

That is the report from headquarters in London. The Germans say that besides the eleven above reported they know that they have sunk the **Warrior** so that makes it twelve, not speaking of the undersea boats. The Germans have lost four ships, and three undersea boats are missing. This is the greatest joy they have had since the war began. To think that they can give England a beating on that her greatest spot – her navy! We often wonder how many men lost their lives. They report here that our loss of life is great but not one third that of the enemy. Well, we must wait and see. I hope we get an English report.

No news of my visit to Ruhleben. Arthur has written to me and expects me daily but I cannot go before Whit week now.

We have had an extra quarter pound of meat this week. Bread has gone up a penny and we are paying six-and-a-half pence for a two pound loaf of very indifferent bread. We are to also have a quarter of butter a week now and not the quarter in fourteen days. So perhaps we shall also get more bread. My servant cannot come out on hers and is always a few days without bread at the end of a fortnight.

So many eatables are not to be had and now we are told that there is no more soda to be had. It is also announced that all cycles and tricycles, or anything with gummi (I mean India rubber), are not to be used for there is to be no more tyres made or repaired.

I had a visit from a friend out of the country today. She lives on a gut (estate) and I asked her the prices of things. She says that they got thirty-five pounds for a very old horse, past work, so it must have been used for slaughtering. They had to give five thousand and five hundred marks for a six-year-old horse for working and that's two hundred and seventy-five pounds in English money. I heard of a horse being sold here for three hundred pounds last week.

Steinoff's son was called up last week and he was the last man in our village between eighteen and forty-five years old.

Arthur wrote last week and mentioned of it being our wedding day. He was only a month too soon. He must lose count of the months in Ruhleben as he did the same last year on my birthday. He made it June and not July.

Frau Voight tells me she went to buy a pair of shoes for her little girl last week. The shoemaker showed her the new stock he had got. Every shoe has a wooden sole of half an inch thick and it is covered with strips of leather half an inch wide and one inch apart. It is like a cross rail across the sole and it does not make so much noise when walking. Still they must be so hard to walk in.

Wednesday 7th June.

We had a sad telegram to read last night. Out of London it is announced that the battleship **Hampshire**, with General Kitchener and all his staff, has struck a mine and all is lost. I cannot believe it. If it is so there are three items for England to face – Kut-Al-Amara with General Townshend, this great sea battle which must have been a German Victory and now this dreadful loss. Up to now we have nothing but the London telegram. In the German papers there is the usual hatred shown and one paper says: 'It took a big coffin for Kitchener – a whole battleship. And he was not worthy of it'.

I think it is so very mean of them to speak of the dead so. The Germans show their hatred so dreadfully. <u>Even</u> the Turks were better. When they took General Townshend they spoke so nicely of his bravery. But not one kind word for Kitchener. There is only hatred and jeers. He was a brave man as well as Townsend.

Saturday 10th June.

Frau Voight and I got ready to go to Berlin today but then we got the news that my papers had been mislaid and that we must wait another week. This is Whit week and strongly observed here so the holidays interfere with the Commandant's work. The police here were very kind and tried all they could. But it was of no use and we hope for better luck next weekend.

No further news of Kitchener. It is reported here that an officer from Hildesheim has sunk the **Hampshire** and has got the Iron Cross for same but I can scarcely believe it. If a big ship like the **Hampshire** was wrecked in a storm then an underwater boat could not do much in the same big sea. It is reported that England had sent out help to the ship but <u>too late</u>. She is known here as '<u>The too late nation</u>'. I am anxious for more news from the English side.

Friday 16th June.

We have sunshine today and it is needed as for two weeks we have had nothing but rain and the gardens are in a sad state.

I go on Sunday to Berlin and can visit Arthur on Tuesday afternoon for one hour. I wonder if I shall find a change in one year and eight months. What a blessing we do not know what is before us. If I had known of this long war from the beginning I think I should have gone mad. With the constant uncertainty and the hope of peace it has only succeeded in making me ill.

No news of importance only the scarcity in food and its dearness. I paid sixpence a pound for flour today and lard is five shillings and ten pence a pound. It is an impossibility to get shoes repaired as there is no leather and you must buy new ones. What we shall do when the stock runs out I do not know. Wear wooden ones very likely.

Yesterday we were astonished to see all the shops (drapers) being closed. They had a government notice to take stock of every yard of stuff they possessed and they have not to sell until they get permission. The prices are to be fixed by the government and so is the quantity of materials to be sold to one person. It will be the same all over the land. I really do not know how it is that we have no failures as the shops are half empty and yet still keep going.

Sunday 25th June.

I was not well on Sunday last when we set off and therefore was not extra well when I met Arthur. We arrived in Berlin at half past five and went to the police at six o'clock (decently civil). On Monday we went to the Commandant at eleven o'clock where we met with our first disappointment. They were very abrupt with us and I was very glad Frau Voight was with me for I could not have managed alone. We were told that we could not visit our husbands more than once and that was to be on a Tuesday for two hours. We begged to be allowed on the Friday but <u>no</u>. Once in three months is all that is allowed.

Tuesday 27th June.

We set off and I was not extra well and our tram went and ran into another so it made me ill. Still I was able to buck up a little before I got to Arthur. He was so delighted to see me and I was very glad to see him looking so well. He is much thinner and looks healthy but his nerves are completely gone. His hands shake like a leaf and he says himself that his nerves are done. He tried to persuade me to go to England but I would not hear of it. Frau Voight got a great shock as her husband looked awfully bad. I should never have recognised him. I was so <u>very, very,</u> sorry for her. She did not give way however until she got back to the hotel. After seeing the great change in her husband I began to think that <u>we</u> have been very lucky. Arthur does not look half as bad. Of course he is busy all day in the post office and it is a great help to the men if they have work. Oh these dreadful times. And what misery we are having at present.

Our visit was so very sad and it was dreadful to meet our husbands in a room of two hundred people with soldiers walking up and down all the time. It was still more dreadful to see them put behind lock and key before we left. We then looked at the crowd of men behind the rails waving their goodbyes to their wives and children. We were lucky in one thing though. It seems that children were not allowed to visit until this week. Whatever should we have done with little Thea Voight

I do not know. Two weeks ago the mothers had brought their children and they were not allowed inside but were left in the care of a soldier outside. Of course they all cried. It must have been so sad to see the little ones without their mothers - and their fathers inside the bars. I am so glad that I did not see that as my impression was bad enough as it was. However it does not do to dwell on it. All in Ruhleben think the war will end this autumn. I do not think so.

Cousin Johanna wrote me that she expected me for a few hours on the Wednesday. I wrote and told her not to send Hedwig for me before five o'clock as I had another engagement. I then went to Schönberg for the evening and came home at ten-thirty.

We spent the remainder of the week shopping and got through a lot of cash. But we could not get anything in the food line because we had no tickets. We found things very scarce in Berlin and a goose of five pounds weight cost twenty-two shillings and sixpence, one egg cost three-and-a- half pence, soap was four shillings and three pence and only on tickets, but each person could have a pound of flour without a ticket at a shilling a pound. A cup of tea is sixpence and a cup of coffee is seven pence Things are awfully dear and fresh vegetables are not to be had at all. This is because Holland has refused to sell any to Germany.

A four-year old child's pair of shoes cost twelve shillings and sixpence and woollen material for a dress, which I have paid often three shillings a yard, is now fifteen shillings a yard. Butter, meat, lard etc. are not to be seen anywhere. We were so pleased to get home and it cost us at least five pounds to see our men for two hours. We were glad of it at the price.

In Berlin things are very bad and one day last week thousands of women went to the palace, very orderly, and asked for bread from the Kaiser. He came out on the balcony and they shouted: 'Give us our men out of the field of battle and more bread'.

The Kaiser answered: 'In two months we shall have a great victory and then there will be peace'.

The women said: 'We want without the battle or the victory. Give to us our men and bread'.

There was no answer to that.

We got home on the Saturday evening of June the 24th and I was so glad to be back again.

Friday 14th July.

It's a long time since I wrote here but there is not much to report.

There is a great deal in the papers about the English offensive in France on the River Somme but the reports are so contradictory one does not know what to believe. In the neutral papers it seems as if England has made advances. The German papers say they are sent back.

Our chief interest is food and this everlasting anxiety is dreadful. When you go to bed you never know if you are to be fed the next day. We have had butter cards for a month but no butter. Remember we are only allowed two ounces per week. A quarter pound must last fourteen days, but at that rate of allowance we are a fortnight without. One sends the maid out every day and it is the same answer: 'None today, come again in three days time'. Now the beer fails. We get a quarter of a pound of meat per week and are very uneasy on a Saturday morning to see if the butcher is open for it can happen that he is closed. Potatoes are very scarce and are thirteen shillings per hundredweight and only so many are allowed per person. The new post tariff comes in on August 1st and everything will be double.

I went to the estate last week but it is no use to gather the fruit for there is so little sugar to preserve it with. We have been allowed a half pound per person per week for a long time, so one cannot preserve much out of that.

Most people think that the war will end next autumn, but I have a poor opinion of it doing so.

Things have been so scarce for so long that one gets used to the shortage and only wonders what will fail us next.

I was so delighted to get on my wedding day, June 30th, a parcel of food stuffs from Arthur. The finest packet I have had for twelve months – one pound of butter, two tins of milk, one pound of biscuits and one pound of tea. It was worth twenty shillings to me.

I am not able to bake now for flour is not sold more than a half pound per week to a person. Before the order I used to get for my cards (bread) the flour and bake myself. I got a little better bread but now that is impossible.

No news from home for four months but Arthur gave me a little home news. I hear of a new baby that is to come to Will and Lilly. I was so very glad to hear that Joan will have a little playmate. I had good news of Ettie and her little ones and also of dad.

Sunday 16th July.

Belle tells me that there is a lot in the neutral papers about the exchange of prisoners (civil) and that it is to be considered. I do not think anything will come of it for

Germany cannot exchange half of hers as they are the children of naturalised English parents. And their wives, children and businesses are here. So how could they exchange them? No, that must wait the end of the war.

It seems as if England has made advances in France, but the papers are very quiet about it. In Russia it is very bad for the Austrians.

My enquartering went away two weeks ago and has never written one line. I do hope nothing has happened to him. He had a dread of Russia having spent one winter there and had been badly wounded. I do hope I hear from him.

Wednesday 19th July.

Went today to Woltershausen and saw on the station a lazarett train being unloaded. It was a dreadful sight and I shall never forget the impression it made on us all. They usually send the wounded here at night but lately there has been so many to come from France that they must unload day as well as night.

We talk often of events and I wish we had other news. Many speak of peace this year. I have no hope of it.

There is such a lot of fruit this year and so very expensive. I wonder at that for no one can preserve as we do not have the sugar. The only reason I can think of the high price is that formerly we had imported fruit. Now it is only our own grown which we have.

Wednesday 26th July.

Yesterday was my birthday and I had lots of good wishes and flowers but not a line from Arthur. I wondered at that because he had written to Belle that he was writing me. James Walmsley wrote me a birthday letter and posted it on the 5th of July in Blackpool and it got here on the 25th. – just the right day. We had a very nice day and Belle made a little tea so we were happy in our own way.

All talk is that no land can hold out this winter and that we are sure of peace before Christmas. I do not feel so hopeful of it myself.

The baths of Salzdetfurth are doing me a lot of good and I feel much better for them.

Friday 28th July.

I received a packet from Arthur today and I was very thankful for the tinned milk and tea. He is well and I can see that he is building up on this exchange of prisoners. But they will never exchange him - he is far too healthy and can do many useful jobs.

Tuesday 1st August.

I had a visit from Johanna Pulmann today. She and her daughter, Hedwig, are staying at Goslar for a few weeks in the hopes of better food. But the feeding is bad there too. It would be funny if it was not so pitiful. When you meet a person and say: 'How do you do?' They reply: 'Do you still get your butter or milk?' Hildesheim is badly off for food and one wonders how much longer these dreadful days last.

When Johanna was here she remarked that England has taken all the German's businesses, land and property from them and she expects it will come here also. If the government takes all our property I shall have to travel home quick. One lives in anxiety from morning until night and does not know what the next day will bring.

I got a new enquarterings today. These last ones are such young men that it is sad to see them.

The drapers are now selling only on permission tickets. Woollen clothes are such a price – twenty-four shillings a yard for cloth that used to be four shillings. I paid fifteen shillings a yard for stuff that was dear at two shillings and eleven pence. The prices of woollen goods are simply awful. A lady told me of paying twenty-five shillings a yard for dress material (wool) and cousin Johanna paid seventeen shillings and sixpence a yard for her stuff. It is really wicked the prices being asked.

Today all bicycle tyres are confiscated. A few weeks ago all bicycles were forbidden to be used and you had to pay a heavy fine if you went for a bicycle ride for pleasure. Now to make sure of it all tyres have to be given up. For a good tyre, inside and outside, you get three shillings; an inferior one is two shillings and for a discarded one sixpence is paid.

It is announced that no more bacon or lard is to be had and that only houses with children are to be served milk. For each child under three you get a pint of milk and over three a gill of milk a day until twelve-years-old, and then no supply at all. We have no children so I am glad of Arthur's cans of milk. Things are fine here.

Thursday 10th August.

Had no letter for two weeks from Arthur and it makes one anxious.

Frau Voight and I hope to travel to Berlin in a few weeks time as it is almost three months since our last visit.

There is a lot in the papers about the confiscation of property in England and I expect daily to hear that all ours is confiscated. What I shall do then I do not know.

Most people are keeping rabbits to kill in the winter so of course the price is very high. A buck and doe of the Belgian breed (coloured like a hare) costs thirty-five shillings a pair, a chicken of eight weeks and not weighing more than one pound costs two shillings and sixpence, a good sized cock or hen that one got for three shillings before the war is now twelve shillings. Eggs are four pence each and you are allowed two per week.

We read that the war can last three years longer. I do not think so.

We had a visit from two gentlemen (brothers) this week and one said the war would last three years longer and the other said Christmas would see the end. There is a great deal of difference in the opinions and a great deal depends on the harvest.

There is to be a house to house examination of food stuffs on the 1st of September. They are to come in your place and see your stock and according to what you have you get your tickets. For instance, if you have thirty eggs in preserve you get no egg tickets until that stock is used up. It is the same for sugar, meats etc. so it is almost impossible for one to stock for the winter.

Monday 14th August.

We have news that our baker is to close. He has done something that is forbidden so his place is closed for an uncertain time. He has been given six days to bake up all his flour and then lock up. It is announced in the papers that it is because he is not dependable. A butcher opposite was done the same about three months ago and is to be allowed to re-open next week. He told a woman that he had no meat and she had a card and money. After that she saw another woman go in and get a parcel. She reported the fact and his punishment for not serving the one that came in first was three months closed shop – rather stiff.

Sunday 20th August.

Got permission to visit Arthur on the 22nd September so I will be in Berlin from the 18th or 19th. It is a pleasure to look forward to. One gets so few of these in war time.

No further news of the exchange of prisoners or the confiscation of goods.

This week we are told that no more sugar is to be obtained until the end of October and one has not been able to save much out of half a pound per person per week. We are allowed (on cards of course) a small packet of saccharine every two weeks – twenty small tablets per person.

We read that all church bells in Vienna are to be melted down for bullets. It will come here soon.

We expect to hear everyday of the arrival of the **Deutschland**, the marvellous underwater boat that got to America. The **Bremen,** the second one, has not yet been announced as arrived and all the people are anxious about it.

The harvest promises to be good but the weather on this date is very cold. Many towns are worse than Hildesheim as regards food, and some a bit better. So we now hear that a set rule is to be made direct from the government and that every town and village is to be served alike.

We read that in England white bread is nine pence for a four pound loaf. That is the price for a dark loaf here and white bread costs one shilling and three pence for four pounds.

Here bacon is six shillings and sixpence a pound when you can get it. One man offered ten shillings a pound for a ham and was refused because it had fat. It was fourteen pounds in weight so you can reckon what that ham would cost. Sugar is four-and-a- half pence a pound, meat is three shillings a pound (with bone) and steak is three shillings and four pence, potatoes are one-and-a-half pence a pound and a cabbage for five people is five pence. Soap is three shillings and three pence and soft soap is three shillings and no more will be made (government orders). We are told that next month is to be the worst during the war for the scarcity of food.

Thursday 24th August.

Great celebrations today for it is announced that the **Deutschland**, the wonderful undersea boat, has returned to Germany. No more does Britain rule the waves as she has nothing to come up to that.

I have no great war news other than the usual German announcement that the enemy is sent back on all fronts and of the usual English and Russian advance made on the frontier. One does not understand half of what is in the papers.

I intend getting a rabbit for a pet so have spoken for one. I hope that I can keep it alive. I have been told that two is far better than one.

I have been to the estate today and had trouble about my potatoes. I do hope that Arthur lets the place before next year as it will be better for all.

We have been told that we must take a census of all our stock and must announce everything we have in the house above one pound weight in the eating line so that they will have an idea of how long this stock will last us. The census is to take place on the 1st of September and anyone falsifying will get one year imprisonment and a fine of twenty pounds. I think very few people have a stock of anything.

Sunday 27th August.

There is a deal in the papers about this exchange of prisoners over forty-five-years-old and Herr Voight has written to his wife that they expect that Herr Droege will be exchanged. If so it will be soon so one does not know how long this uncertainty will last. Perhaps I shall be amongst my own before Christmas.

They are all concerned about this food census, because the rain has increased these last few days and it is bad for the harvest.

We are told also that during the month of September we are to receive papers to fill up stating how much money each person has invested in foreign countries. It is not for taxation but to get at the amount of German money there is in foreign lands. I told Belle that I thought it a sign of peace much more eloquent than lectures. But one must wait and see.

I got news of likelihood to clear out and Mrs. Voight is thinking of taking an etage (a floor) as she is sick of hotel life. I shall be glad to hear of what Arthur thinks about it all.

We are all earnestly requested to take all our old gold ornaments to the town hall and we shall be given the market price for it. A lady of my acquaintance took a lot of old family jewellery, gold watches, chains, broaches and got sixteen pounds for them. She was very pleased at the price besides feeling that she was helping the Fatherland.

The children are to go from house to house and beg old bottles, jars, rags, paper or anything at all in the lumber line and for a certain monies worth, gathered by one school, will get a free holiday for a whole day. Every child has been gathering cherry, plum, apricot and peach stones for they contain oil. When the children gather a certain weight they are taken to the school and prizes or a holiday given. They have it so finely reckoned that every twenty-eight cherry stones give half a tea spoonful of oil (pure). You can imagine the amount of stones gathered.

A friend of ours has had her son missing for a long time but has now heard that he is in Siberia. He has now written home for a grammar book as he is learning Russian and Polish.

Another friend, Frau Pestorrous, got a parcel yesterday and on opening it out fell her only son's watch, scapular and rosary. In the next post she got a letter to announce his death and one also from Luni (her son). He was just one day at the front when shot in the head.

One ceases to wonder at the sad things we hear daily and only wonders how the relatives manage to live through it all. I know numerous families personally who have lost every male member of the entire family. Five or six cousins of the one name fell in a month. The family completely died out for not one had married.

Monday 28th August.

We read startling news today. Italy declares war on Germany and Romania declares war on Austria. Everyone is astonished. The news from Romania was so favourable last week. We had a telegram last night that the first Romanian prisoners had been taken. I wonder if it will prolong or end the war.

The weather has been very wet and cold this past two weeks and it is bad for the potatoes and most of the corn is ripe.

Wednesday 30th August.

Had a letter from Arthur to say that he is full of hope that he is to be released and that he has to go to England. I expect that he will write instructions to me. I do not know how to arrange it and would like someone to speak to about it. Perhaps the exchange will not take place before my visit of the 22nd of September.

They make light here of the two new war declarations, but thoughtful people say that there are many people with money in Romania and it will be serious from that point of view. It will also be serious in the fact of food buying. Some even say that Germany had no need to declare war on them at all.

Every day we are having rain and I think that it will be bad for the potatoes for the earth is so very cold and wet for August.

Friday 1st September 1916.

We have had many surprises last month and I wonder if this month will bring the same amount. The people say that Greece and Denmark are very unsettled.

I went to Hannover yesterday having got police permission. In one shop a man came in and after asking for several things which he was not able to obtain. He remarked: 'Now all our prayers must be that Holland

and the Swiss remain neutral or we shall be in a fix. In fact I think it is over with us'.

Different people have different ideas but most are very downhearted about Romania. Another remarked: 'I wish they would end the war by coming in. And I don't care which way at all'.

Frau Voight says that her husband has written to her and says that the exchange of prisoners has already commenced and that Arthur is writing instructions to me. I do hope all is in order for his exchange. I still hope he will be there for me to see on the 22nd. I wonder if they would allow that I visited earlier if it should be by chance that he goes home.

Things look very bad for the winter.

Monday 4th September.

Arthur says that he has every hope of exchanges and wants to wait in Holland for me to join him. That's awkward as I have much to arrange first. I go to Berlin on the 20th so it is not too long to wait now.

The fifth war loan is in force and they say it is not going very well.

Tuesday 12th September.

I had a letter from Willie and it was written on April 1st so it had taken five months and ten days to come here. It came from America and all were well when it was written and it is my latest news from home.

Soldiers go away each day and there is a big talk of a great offensive to be made on the English in Flanders. Hindenburg has been made General Field Marshal and has gone to France.

The people here talk a lot of a new forced war loan. It appears that this 5th war loan is not going so well. So they say. After it is closed up there will come the forced loan and everyone must pay into it. You will be forced to do so. I myself cannot see it, but am told it is to be so.

Great scandal is talked here about Romania. It appears that a great deal of fodder for the cattle was bought there a few days before the declaration of war and it has all been found to be poisoned. Cattle are dying off and it is also said that a box of pudding powders was also poisoned. I can only think that it is gossip. It is very dangerous talk and the people are so very angry about it. What a dreadful thing it will be if it is all lies for I can scarcely credit it being true.

One gets such dreadful things in the papers these days and this last visit of the Zeppelins to England has been terrible according to our papers. I wonder if they have really done such damage.

We read also that in England boys of seventeen-years-old are not called up into the military service and also those over forty years of age. It makes me wonder so much about them all at home as news is so very scarce.

Saturday 16th September.

The Romanian poisoning is found now not to be true. Perhaps it was put in the papers to give the people something to talk about.

Arthur has written and given me an address to stay at in Berlin. I will go there on Wednesday the 20th and visit him on Friday afternoon. I have such a lot to tell him and two hours is not half long enough for me.

We had news from the Kaiser today and he himself has telegraphed that the Romanians have had a dreadful beating though it has resulted in the loss of Prince Frederick William of Hesse. The people here are so very hard of belief now and they say that this telegram has been published to let the people have more faith in the news. It is because they do not believe the official notes. Also it is a lift to the new war loan for it is not being paid up as it should be. The people are more interested in the food question because the weather is so bad for the harvest. The potatoes up to now are not good and we have not heard the result of the corn harvest.

It has been publicly announced that all people must have electric light in their houses for there will be no oil this year. Electric or gas must be put in so we must put the Steinoffs a light in the place. In most villages there is electric power for threshing, so now the people must have the light in their houses and barns. That is where this land has an advantage as they do not need coal for gas and power.

Most of the electric works are driven by the water power, so it is a very great saving of coal and Germany has not so many gas works as England. Germany has gone straight from petroleum lamps to electric light. Here in Hildesheim there are few homes with gas and all are lamps or electric. People cook, iron and wash all with electric.

The new time is to be changed on the 1st of October because now it is not so light in the mornings and it is too cold for the children to go to school at seven o'clock when it is really only six o'clock. These past few weeks it has been cold and wet and is real autumn weather.

It is announced today that next week we get tickets, on application from the town hall, for sugar for preserving and we are to have a pound a head. We can't do much with that. It is impossible to buy a pound of jam at present and the last that was sold was all sorts mixed up together. It was half turnips and now I cannot even get that. Fruit is there in plenty, but no sugar. Plums are plentiful so we eat stewed fruit. I did buy the saccharine but it was dreadful to use and tastes awful. We are told that there are three hundred chickens to be sold today at one-and-a-half pounds weight and are to cost five shillings and sixpence each and are sold by the government. Eggs are four pence each and you get two per week and most always I eat my half a quarter of butter in two days so I am five days without. It is not at all pleasant.

I have had nice fruit from the estate this week and have got permission from the government to have my potatoes from the estate also. That is a blessing.

Tuesday 26th September.

I travelled to Berlin on the 20th of this month and saw Arthur in Ruhleben on the 22nd. We had only a short stay but pleasant. We came home on the 23rd. I found him looking very well but he has not much faith in the exchange of prisoners. He believes there will be no exchange now until all are exchanged. If he is sent home then I shall have to go also. The uncertainty is awfully unpleasant. The visit did not make such a bad impression this time as I knew what to expect, so it was not so bad. Arthur gave me some butter and soap and I was very thankful for it. I wonder why they do not send him some from home.

Things are very bad in Berlin in the eating line and we never got butter or sugar on the table in the hotel. You got tea or coffee and three small thin pieces of bread off a four pound loaf. A pot of jam was on the table and it was all this mixed up together jam. For sugar there was saccharine that had been dissolved in water. A small bottle of this sweet water was on every table and you put a teaspoonful of it in your cup of tea. I was sorry that I had not brought a little sugar with me. Butter I found none to buy and eggs were seven pence each. Mrs. Voight paid that for some eggs for Thea. The servants in the hotel say that they have not had butter or sugar for over two months.

On our return here we found that the potatoes were sold out and the people running all over Hildesheim looking for them. The potato harvest is very bad and I am very much afraid for the coming winter. However, the bakers were told to give four pounds of bread on the ten pound potato card so the people had something to eat. There is a deal of grumbling and people seem to want peace at any price now that the food is so very scarce.

Monday 2nd October.

No more doubt about the potato harvest, it is terribly bad, and our allowance of potatoes has been reduced to one-and-a-half pounds per day per person. I am so sorry for the people. The fruit has also been confiscated for a few days until the wants of the army have been satisfied. It is quite right that the soldiers have to be attended to first and I am sure that no one thinks otherwise. So many people do think that the fruit is held back for other purposes. I have nothing to do with that business for I get all mine from the garden.

I am glad to say that I have let the house and garden at last and I have now only the orchard to attend to. I am sure it is for the best.

Sunday 22nd October.

I have been to the estate and hear that the Germans are leaving Belgium and the people say that is a sign of peace. There is no doubt that the people's thoughts are on peace because we really have famine staring us in the face.

One notices the people going thinner and paler. If one of the old people takes ill he very rarely get better.

The food question is <u>very</u> serious. We have been six weeks and never seen an egg. Fat of any sort is not to be had and on a diet of two ounces of butter a week one cannot cook anything now that we have no milk. I did ask for half a gill every morning but no it was not to be had. I bought a goose last Saturday because I could get a little fat from it. It was ten pounds in weight and cost me forty-four shillings. It just does not seem true. Forty-four shillings for a bird for dinner! Three of us had dinner for two days off it and then I preserved the remainder in glasses for another day.

I have bought a few fowls, eight in all, and am feeding them up. Then I also have my two rabbits. One does all kinds of things for its dinner.

Things are so very scarce and even things you have cards for you do not get. Now it is the vegetables – carrots, cabbage etc. Since the potatoes are so scarce, also so bad, one must cook other things. In one day the vegetables doubled in price. Carrots that cost eight pfennigs, about one penny, suddenly rose to two pence and one could not buy them at all as they were all sold out. Cabbage and swedes that were sold at a penny a pound are now two pence and such crowds awaiting their turn to buy.

Arthur has written today that he has been photographed and has also written to England for my birth certificate. So it looks like as if I am to go at last. Everyone is astonished at the news but all wish me luck.

I am sorry to leave some of the very nice friends I have made and I think that they are sorry to lose me.

Thursday 26th October.

Alice Graeinghoff has been to see me and came to give me some messages to take to her sisters regarding her mother's death. It is very sad to think of it all as I was very fond of Mrs. Durselen. From what Alice says, things are not very bad in Königswinter as food is more plentiful being nearer to the frontier. She does not think that I shall travel before the December boat which is on the 6th. She says that the exchange will last some time yet.

Hermenia says that if a great offensive is not made in a few weeks then the war will last a long time. Every one longs for peace here. Things are so very bad in the food line and also the clothes.

I have been able to get the old servant of Uncle George to come to us and I think I can leave her here and she will attend to Belle whilst I am in England. I do wish that I could leave things a little more in order for her but it is impossible to do more.

Monday 6th November.

Up to now there is no further news of my journey only that a friend tells me that he would not cross the water because the German undersea boats are now in the channel. They will sink everything in the shape of a boat. It is not at all pleasant.

I have written to Arthur and told him that I prefer to stay here and visit him at Christmas and then perhaps cross on the 6th of January. I have no faith in him being exchanged so very soon.

I have written also to Willie today. I do worry often about my brothers for I know nothing of them. Also of Ettie and Kittie, I seem to know nothing of their lives and my own is just dragging out an existence. Will these days never end? One hopes each day to read of being a little nearer the end, but it is as far away as ever. Perhaps after Romania is settled it will be soon put in sight again.

The food question is very serious and I am so thankful for Arthur's presents. If we are to get a pint of milk a day we are to have no butter. So it is either butter or milk. The potatoes are scarcer and we only get seven pounds for six days now. When one gets a few diseased ones then the portion is too small. Oil, fat or margarine is not to be had at all. Meat we have one day a week and we have had no eggs for a long time and the fish is awfully dear. I paid two shillings and eight pence last week for codfish and mackerel is three shillings a pound. A sixpenny tin of sardines is now one shilling and sixpence and all other fish is not to be had. Rice is four shillings a pound, flour sixpence a pound, soap, awful stuff, is three shillings and sixpence and the poor cannot buy it at all. We now get half-a-pound of sugar in fourteen days. We can buy twenty tablets of saccharine for twenty pfennigs and a mark. We use that for tea and cook with the sugar.

I am glad Arthur gets his parcels from England as I cannot send him anything from here. He tells me that he regularly gets a parcel from Uncle Frank MacMorragh, also James Walmsley and occasionally from others. It is a grand job they do to remember the interned ones. I am so thankful.

Monday 13th November.

I have no further news of my leaving here and the police tell me that they have no word yet from the Commandant's. It sounds as if the question is not settled yet.

Every day I get from Holland the 'Daily Telegraph' and for this I pay fourteen shillings a month. I read nothing in it at all about the exchange.

Clemens Peligeaus came in on Saturday and said that he had read in the Köln paper that in Amsterdam they were waiting for eight hundred prisoners out of Ruhleben on Thursday to England.

This morning Frau Voight got a letter from her husband from Ruhleben and it said: 'We have heard nothing definite of the exchange of the forty-five-year-old ones yet, but let's hope that it is before Christmas'. I am going to take it as it comes.

They talk a lot of Norway and also of Wilson being elected again. They say of the latter that it does not matter to Germany who is elected as neither is her friend.

Potatoes are still the topic and plenty of homes have been five and six days without one to eat. When one remembers that it is the staple food and bread is only allowed at half-a-pound per day it is very serious.

A visitor here was only too glad to take enough away with her for her supper; and that on a Thursday afternoon. Parcels do not count at all now. We are allowed one gill of skimmed milk per day and no more and fresh milk is only for children under six years of age.

I went to a school today to help wash the children. It is a kindergarten school and a very fine institution they have here. The children are from two-years-old up to being able to go to school and are taken care of in the town. It is a building all on its own and a lady caretaker lives there with a cook. The children come in at half past eight in the morning and bring their lunches with them. They get a plate of thick soup at noon and leave at half past four. Their parents pay twenty pfennigs a day for it and twice a week they are bathed. That is what I go for. We have a fine bathroom with plenty of towels and we do so many children per day – ten to twelve. Carole Osthaus and I go together two mornings a week. Two other ladies do the same and there is another morning for bathing. There are in all fifty to sixty children in this school and in the town there are four such places. The children are so happy and every accommodation is there for them – an open air playroom, a sleeping room and a winter playroom. One is really surprised at the details attended to. One little fellow said to me: 'Are you our new bath lady?'

None are at all afraid of the water. Many are very poorly clad but the greater portion comes from very comfortable homes.

Wednesday 15th November.

Got a letter from Arthur yesterday in which he writes that he expects me to travel to England on the 6th of

December and gives me the name of a lady, a Mrs. Ferguson, who is also to travel on that day. Now, this morning I got a letter from the Commandant who tells me that the exchange of prisoners over forty-five is not yet complete and may last some weeks before the final arrangements. If one only knew what to do for the best. However I have written to Arthur to say that I can be ready to travel on the 6th. I feel terribly nervous over the journey but shall not be alone.

We read of a terrible battle in France, north of Combles, and the papers here say that our losses were heavy. So it must have been very bad. We also read that we are to eat swedes instead of potatoes as a substitute. I am afraid that they will not be as satisfying as potatoes but I am sure they will be just as healthy and nutritious.

I also saw a letter from a prisoner in England. He is in Handforth and is named Cosie. He writes very brightly and says he is in the best of health.

Then I hear of one in the Isle of Man who writes that they do not have enough to eat and that the water comes through the roof as they lie in bed. I can scarcely believe that, but his people assure me it is so and that the prisoners live the whole year in tents.

There was an announcement yesterday that every man up to the age of sixty-years-old, and every <u>woman</u> also, will be called on to work for the government. It will be on ammunition or some other employment. They tell us that we will not be beaten by England for every woman and man there will be working for the war. People wonder what it means for women are already doing men's work and have been for eighteen months now.

Things are bad for Christmas with no cocoa or chocolate to be got. A woman was speaking to me yesterday and she has had no bread for three whole days. She had eaten her fourteen day portion in ten days. When I asked what she will do, she replied: 'We must do it. There is nothing else for us. What can we do against it if there is not enough bread and potatoes for us?'

I do admire their patience. I often wonder if the English people are suffering hunger and cold to help their government. <u>And so very patiently.</u>

Friday 17th November.

I have been to the estate today to say adieu to the people. They have no idea that I am going to England and think I am only not coming anymore before spring. I think that all is in order with the house now and I am glad that it is let at last.

It is surprising how many women are doing the work in these country stations. There is not a man to be seen on the stations or on the post or trams.

Saturday 18th November.

We have news today of the flyer over Munich and his dropping of three bombs. But there were no casualties. Also of the accident to the **Deutschland,** but it is not serious.

Rosie v.d. Busch has come for a few days and I am so glad to see her as she is so very chatty and friendly. She told me of Joedecke in our village who would not send any more potatoes to the government than he thought fit. He kept all that he thought he required. One day six soldiers came and broke into his potato cellar (it was locked) and weighed out his quantity of potatoes. They left him one-and-a-half per day per person until next harvest and took <u>all</u> the remainder. They then sent him a bill for the work he had caused them. There is a way of making you do things here. He cannot work with that allowance of potatoes until next July because farmers eat at least three pounds a day.

Many more soldiers are called up and in one class at Josephenun School only two scholars are left as all the others were over eighteen years and have gone to the military.

Wednesday 22nd November.

Got a letter from Arthur today in which he says that it is not at all certain that Mrs. Ferguson travels on the 6th. If that is so I shall not go because I feel that I cannot make the journey alone. Perhaps she will travel in January.

Arthur writes me that he has had a letter from Ettie and she says that Bob must go to the military in December and she wishes that I was there. So do I. If only I could get over to help them all in this dreadful time.

Tomorrow is general holiday here for the Catholics as it is St. Elizabeth's feast and for the Protestants a day of penance so we keep it as a Sunday.

I got some honey today at four shillings a pound and was glad to get it. It takes the place of sugar.

Friday 24th November.

No further news of my journey so I think it very improbable that I travel to England on the 6th.

I think so much of father, Winnie and Ettie and wish I was able to help them.

We have had further advice from a friend in a good position and he strongly advises me to remain here. He says that Hildesheim is much better than a Zeebruggen prison and that a ship with passengers from Holland to England had been taken there. If only one knew what to do for the best.

We are told now that the eating places for the poor (like our soup kitchens) are to be two days a week without food. It means that the people cannot buy any portion with potatoes in it for two days each week. They must eat barley cooked with apples or plums. These kitchens are a fine institution for the poor. You can eat there (must take your own spoon) or buy it in a dish and eat it at home. Many people send their servants to buy one for fifty pfennigs (sixpence) and all the family eat the same. It is all cooked together like a thin potato hash. Sometimes it is potatoes and cabbage and other times it is potatoes and carrots or swedes. Twice a week there is a little meat in and on Friday it is fish. You get so many potatoes and half a herring or a few mussels cooked with the potatoes. These kitchens have of course been provided for the winter with vegetables and, as many houses are without, the people must all buy their food there. The food is cooked and served by ladies or women who give their time for nothing. Each person takes their own spoon and meals are served from half past eleven to half past two, and from six to eight o'clock. All is in a thin soup and no knifes and forks are required.

There is talk of instituting a better class of place so that the better class people can go and eat. They will pay a little more for their food and then the profits will go to the kitchen.

We read about the death of the Emperor of Austria and wonder if it will alter the war at all.

From here many journeymen were sent away this week and all were eighteen-years-old. In the better schools the entire top classes fail pupils.

In the November muster of military over six hundred were sent from the young scouts of this town. They seemed only children when gathered together at the station. So many mothers are so sad with the children being taken straight from school and to the shooting graves.

Rosie has returned to Celle but she comes again in a couple of weeks to spend Christmas with us. Of course she must bring all her food with her, potatoes, sugar, jams and her bread and meat cards. She writes us this morning that the town of Celle is in darkness at eight o'clock each evening and that the gas goes out in each house at the same time (nine o'clock on Saturdays). It is to save gas and coal. Here it is one hour later. The houses with electric light are better off though we are all advised to go to bed earlier and save light to help the Fatherland.

Thursday 7th December.

I had hoped this time last month that I was on my way home but it's not to be. I go next week to visit Arthur and hope that I find him well again.

Yesterday we got new orders (the outlanders) and if we are found in the streets after eight o'clock at night or before seven in the morning without written permission from the police we can be put in prison. We must all be in our houses at that time so my two nights a week at Frau Voight's is at an end. She cannot leave Thea and visit me. I used to take my sewing and sit with her from eight o'clock to ten o'clock so now it is goodbye to all that.

We celebrate tonight the fall of Bucharest. The poor Romanians are completely beaten and all our flags are flying and the bells are ringing. How do those people feel who are terribly so beaten? It must be awful.

They tell us here that it is a wonderful gain of food stuffs and oil so perhaps we will get a little extra. I ordered a gill of oil yesterday for twelve shillings a gill. A goose now costs six shillings a pound so one of twelve pounds costs three pounds twelve shillings. The rich people pay it.

Well, if Romania is such a gain as they say we can hope to have more flour, potatoes and meat and not the everlasting swedes.

Hermenia was here yesterday and bought one pound of wool at twenty-six shillings per pound and gets four pairs of stockings. And she has to knit them herself. I thought it was awful when I must pay twenty-five shillings and sixpence a yard for a dress that used to cost seven shillings but the price of this wool is much more out of proportion. It used to be three shillings and sixpence per pound and the shop man said it will be thirty shillings next month.

This new civil service comes at once into force - men from seventeen to sixty and women from seventeen to fifty. They have built a quantity of new ammunition works in the centre of Holland and now want workers for them. I as an Englander do not count.

Saturday 9th December.

Not any further news of the gains we are to get from Romania but it is a fine thing for Germany.

All plain chocolate is now confiscated and so it is goodbye to any extra for Christmas. The last cost nine

shillings a pound. I bought today a little for Christmas –
wine etc. and the prices are enough to stagger one.
Almonds are eight shillings a pound and used to be one
shilling and three pence, brandy is twenty-one shillings
and cheap port wine (Tarragona) that used to be a
shilling a quart is now three shillings and sixpence for a
three gill bottle. No more bread than half-a-pound per
day is to be fixed for Christmas, and no more than one
pound of potatoes. We hope for more than a quarter
pound of meat that week because there are three
Sundays together. Everything is confiscated. You can buy
nothing that is necessary without a note from the
government; not even a pocket handkerchief or a pair of
gloves. All is under control.

We are wondering how we shall find it in Berlin.
Of course, we shall take some bread, butter and sugar
with us.

A funny thing happened last night. A soldier came
here and asked if I had yet gone to England and also if
my man was free. He said that a lady had sent him but
he did not know her name. He was told to say: 'A certain
lady wished to know it'. It sounds very funny.

No further news of the exchange and I expect to be in
Berlin in a few days.

Wednesday 13th December.

Frau Voight, Thea and I arrived in Berlin. Things have
changed since our last visit and it is sad to see the place.
Everyone is talking of peace terms but very few are
hopeful. They remark that if one only knew the contents
of the Kaiser's note then one could judge. It came as a
great surprise, this peace announcement, though many

said it is only to keep the people quiet until after the New Year. I think that the scarcity of food has a great deal to do with it. It was very noticeable in Berlin that no potatoes were to be got and women workers were everywhere. They were waiters, drivers, window cleaners, tram conductors, parcel deliverers and navvies, in fact everything. I must say what struck me most was to see women repairing a water burst in the street. They were just like regular navvies pulling up tram lines, laying pipes and digging clay.

We heard at the Commandant's that just half an hour before we arrived permission had been granted to the people who only visit once in three months (that is from a distance) that they can visit their husbands in Ruhleben twice in the week. We decided to stay eight days in Berlin and visit our husbands on Friday and Tuesday and then return home on Wednesday the 20th of December. Our men did not know of the extra visit and were delighted. Arthur is in the picture of health thanks to the English food and is very hopeful of the exchange. He strongly urges me to go home in February. I scarcely know what to do as I am so afraid of the journey.

Arthur tells me that some of the men have taken the disappointment of the exchange very much to heart as they had built themselves up so on being home for Christmas.

Here one remarks the change of the men very much. The soldiers are either very young or very old. The only fine soldiers one meets are the soldiers who are home on leave.

We thought to do some Christmas shopping but it was no use. Everything was sold on cards and as we were not residents we had no cards for the Berlin shops. If you buy a costume you have to give up the old one. If you want a pair of shoes you have to give up the old ones. It is impossible to get one article (a pair of gloves etc.) without a ticket saying that you have permission. Each article is booked to you and you may not buy two of anything only fancy work. I mean handwork that you do yourself.

Hotels must be coining it in as four tablespoons of vegetables costs two shillings and sixpence and beer is nine pence a pint. So we drink wine. It is impossible for things to last another year at this rate.

Sunday 17th December.

We went to Wilmersdorf, a suburb of Berlin, to visit Herr Schumacher. He is a brother of Frau Voight, but we got confused in the number so we had to go again on Monday and we had a very nice time there. He is a painter and had been interned for two years. He showed us many sketches of Ruhleben. He has changed his nationality and he intends to make Berlin his home. He is now free but expects to be called up for military duty any day. Everyone tells him he was a fool to come out to the scarcity of food. He confesses that it was better in Ruhleben and says he misses his friends very much and at times feels very lonely.

We made our second visit to Ruhleben on Tuesday and had a famous cup of coffee and some jam puffs baked by Herr Voight. They were splendid. It is so wonderful what men can do when put to it. He was very proud of them and we encouraged his work by eating them up. We ladies got a fine parcel for which we were very thankful.

We were glad to return home and now we have seen Ruhleben in summer, autumn and winter and hope it is our last visit. It makes one sad to leave them there and it always makes me think of caged up animals.

Belle and Rosie met me on my return at the Hildesheim station. Rosie is staying with me until the New Year and I am glad of her company. Frau Voight and her sister Thea are also coming for one evening this feast time.

Christmas Day.

We have just finished our dinner and have had such a nice hare. It was a present from a gentleman to me. I have many good friends. We got up early this morning and all went to six o'clock mass at the Dom, received Holy Communion, heard three masses and then returned here for breakfast. We each put our surprises on our chairs under a serviette and were a very merry party of three for a few minutes. It touched me to see how very much Rosie and Belle had thought for me. I had such a number of surprises, useful and ornamental, and among several from Belle was a very nice broach which her husband had brought for her from India. It was a blue and white sapphire set in the form of a fly. It was very kind of her to give it to me and I am very proud of it. I admire stones so much.

Arthur had written to Belle to get me something for him and she bought me a lovely black Spanish lace shawl or scarf. Rosie gave me, among other things, a very pretty travelling writing case and cushion. Herr Schumacher sent me a fine etching of the Juden Strasse which is a street in Hildesheim. Frau Voight, Fil

Schumacher, Hermenia all tried to make my Christmas happy. I have so many kind friends that I can never forget.

I spent Christmas Eve at the Voights as they had a tree and we tried to make as much of a feast as possible. We could not get any chocolate, or biscuits, and cakes have not been made for some time. We are all forgetting how to eat several things and eggs are never seen. I do not know how the poor manage as here it is dreadful and yet not as bad as in Berlin and the big towns.

We got no extra meat but we got half-a-pound of flour each to bake with, but no fat. We only get one pound of sugar a month per person now and eat principally swedes. The five pounds of potatoes per two weeks is not enough, but I have more for I get them from the estate.

I had a letter from Arthur on the 30th and he says that it has been officially announced that the exchange commences in a couple of weeks time. I must send his clothes etc. and get my papers ready to go. I hope that he is right but all my friends say that I am foolish and must stay here. It makes me quite nervous of the journey.

I shall enquire at the police this week if I must travel when I receive my papers even if Arthur does not leave this month. I would rather meet him in Rotterdam and then travel home together. But perhaps it would be better and safer for us to travel separately for surely a ship which contains exchange prisoners will be certain to reach the English shores safely.

One dares not think of the shipping accidents which have happened this year.

I know I am glad to say "goodbye" to 1916 and hope it is not my luck to have such another year of suspense during my life. But one never knows.

New Year's Day January 1st 1917.

Another weary year is at an end and one wonders what the new one will bring to us. Peace does not seem any nearer but one can never tell. It does not do to look back on all the misery one has lived through. There are many more sad homes this Christmas.

A lady said to me: 'I am tired of trying to comfort the people and do not wonder when they grumble so'. She is a good soul but her patience is getting to an end. I myself cannot see the people lasting another year on this food supply, but they say: 'What can we do but sit down to it all?'

It is the little ones that grieve me. Please God it is the last New Year's Day that dawns with such misery in the world.

Sunday 7th January.

Today is Belle's birthday so we made a feast day of it. She had a lot of callers and we had plum pudding for dinner. We then drank champagne and tried to cheat ourselves into thoughts of peace.

The Kaiser's note addressed to the soldiers was published yesterday. He says he has offered the hand of peace, but England and her allies refused to accept it. So now it is to be war to the knife.

One dreads the coming year with this awful hate between nations.

We have not heard anything from Arthur since 30th December so I do not know if he has received any more news of his exchange.

We hear that we are to have only half-a-pound of potatoes per day per person commencing on January 5th

and that is dreadful when one thinks that there is no more bread given than half-a-pound per day. No-one can live on half-a-pound of bread and half-a-pound of potatoes per day. We have only one quarter of sausage and one quarter of meat with bone per week and now we are to have only three-quarters of sugar per person per month. We get two ounces of tea and coffee at stated times. The last was at Christmas and it was two months since the last sale. Toilet soap is not to be had at all and a very dreadful scouring soap is three shillings and sixpence a pound.

Tuesday 9th January.

I have written up to Berlin today for my permission to travel to England. One does not know which way to turn for advice and everyone tells me to stay here - at least my life is safe. Arthur says I must go at once on February 6th.

Well, I am getting ready. I have sent him some things to pack and he says he can send them in a case. I hope so. I have plenty of luggage but only clothes are allowed. Arthur's gold watch I also sent today.

I took some shoes to be repaired for him but it is impossible to get them done. First the leather fails and then the new shoes are dreadful to obtain. The poor little ones, their feet are in such a sad way what with stockings and shoes failing. If I was a poor mother here I think I should go mad. It's just the same with the food. Everywhere you go the people are talking about food. In the trams, in the trains, in the shops the only thing you hear is: 'We have had no butter in our house for three days'.

'We are quite without bread and I do not know where to buy anything for a substitute'.

'If only I had twenty pounds of potatoes. It does not matter what it costs'.

'What are you having in your house for dinner?'

'Have you got enough bread at your home for a bit for lunch?'

They ask this at ten o'clock in the morning. The talk on food is everlasting.

Wednesday 10th January.

We went to the theatre to see 'Puss in Boots'. A poor show when one has seen English pantomimes, but we enjoyed it pretty fair. Many children were there for it was the last performance this year.

Thursday 11th January.

I have been to Mrs. Voight's to tea today and we had some very nice English biscuits and tea. We have to go again to Dr. Gearland about our passports as they are not quite in order. I have a good reason for leaving but Mrs. Voight has not. Her husband is not being exchanged and she is leaving only for financial reasons. I wonder if they will accept that in Berlin. We were introduced to a Miss Meyrego there. She is really of French extraction, but was born in England so she has to announce herself twice a week to the police. I quite like her and hope I shall see her again.

Today we also hear of the serious state of the towns for coal. The coal is there but there are no men to get it for us as all are at the front. Many schools are closed because they cannot be heated. If you want coal you go to the town hall and report when you last had any and how much and then a man comes to see the state of your cellar. The price is not much dearer at only two shillings and two pence per hundredweight but you cannot get it at all. I say that we should all lie in bed to keep ourselves warm and then we would not require so much heat or food.

I go twice a week again to the school to bathe the children and it is remarkable how much better dressed they are since Christmas. It is the result of all the Christmas charities and the little ones have profited very much. Ladies have made all kinds of underwear for them from all sorts of cloth. Materials of all colours and all qualities are joined together and the result is that the children are all warmer and neater. They are also cleaner because their mothers have the old ones to change into while the new ones are being washed. It is very praiseworthy to see the mending and the time that has been spent on the little garments. But still I must take my own soap.

We have had no fresh fish for two weeks now. I have bought some 'Finnie haddock' - a rather large fish and cost three shillings and sixpence a pound. I wonder how it will taste.

I was very thankful for Arthur's parcel and we had a tin of salmon for dinner, because the fish here is so strongly smoked that we must soak it in water for four hours before cooking.

Friday 12th January.

I got a letter from Arthur this morning that he wrote on the 7th. It has taken a long time to come. He tells me that he has his papers and hopes that I have seen to mine. He also gives me some general instructions about going to the border. I shall write to him tonight about it. He seems to have great hopes of getting away soon. Again I have my doubts of it.

Monday 15th January.

I had a visit yesterday from a Frau Winslov and she seemed surprised that the newspapers I receive give so much news of food stuffs. She had the opinion that it was just as bad in England as here for supplies. She also expressed her doubts as to the government allowing me to travel. She said that I could say so much of the shortages. I laughed as I told her that the English papers could tell me news of various provinces of Germany four days before I heard of it myself. It was published in the English papers how much butter, meat and potatoes were reduced in weight in the big cities. I gave her the date of the newspaper in which it appeared. She was astonished.

We read in a neutral paper today that Greece is on the English side and has accepted all her terms. If this is so, how can the tale be true that we are told? We are told that all the foodstuffs that Germany got in Romania she had to send to the Greeks to help them in the blockade that England had commenced around Greece. I think myself that there were no gains from Romania and that the tale of help to Greece was a fib.

I read in the paper of the appalling Christmas weather in Manchester with such a dreadful fog everywhere. Well, even the thoughts of a fog made me feel homesick. Perhaps I shall be enjoying one in March.

I have just seen a lot of Belgian and Siberian prisoners go past. Poor fellows, they look so downcast. I know just how they feel.

I think of the Germans in England and hope it lies in my power to do one of them a good turn. I also hope their lot is a better one than these ones. I cannot think that the English are at all spiteful to a prisoner. What can the poor man do? It's the multitudes and bad governments that caused this dreadful war.

We read dreadful accounts in the papers of what is to take place in the next few months. Nothing is to be spared on land, or sea, and by all accounts all kinds of frightfulness are to be practised. I do hope that England will not resort to anything, but a clean fair fight. It is better to lose with honour than win with disgrace for her children to carry forever. But we are not our own masters. We have to obey orders and it is sad for any country when a man in command has no respect for honour.

Thursday 18th January.

We had a very heavy snowfall last night and all the children are so very happy in the snow. Sledges and toboggans are all over the place and everywhere looks so very pretty. All the trees bowed down with snow and the silence seems such a relief. Nothing can be heard but sleigh bells and the laughing children. The little ones have not a thought of these dreadful times in their pleasures of the snowfall.

I met Mrs. Herald today and she tells me that she has let her house to three gentlemen - prisoners from Belgium. They are bankers and have had to leave their homes. They are men of over forty-five-years-old and look very well fed.

No news of Arthur's leaving, but I read in the English papers that the exchange is to commence at once.

Tuesday 23rd January.

Had a letter from Arthur on the 19th and he says that he has not any definite news of his release but wishes me to go on the 6th February. My papers are not yet here from Berlin.

We are having dreadfully cold weather and for three days now it has been twelve degrees below freezing and all the pipes are frozen up.

We are told that we will get more bread when the swedes are done. A nice prospect but we do not say anything about it.

Churches and most schools are not treated as coal is so scarce and there are no men to do the digging for it.

The war news is very quiet, but we read of the Kaiser telling his people that he was the only worthy man to offer peace but no one will take it. So it is to be another dreadful year of losses. Now all the people say that the war will last at least another year.

Many of my friends have been to see me before I fly away from them. They say that they have many messages for anxious friends.

I wrote to Arthur today to try to get two masses said in Ruhleben for my mother and his brother Marcus. Here it is impossible to get one said as there are so many dead people to say masses for and so many priests away.

Pastor Gruse came to say goodbye on Saturday. He is from Alsace and at last has permission to travel home after being a war prisoner for one year and nine months, because now they have found he is innocent.

Thursday 25th January.

I am busy paying farewell calls and getting ready for my journey.

We heard yesterday at Sermes, where we had a cup of tea, of a sea battle but it must have been only a slight encounter for there is not much news of it in the papers.

Arthur wrote me today and says a few more people are leaving Ruhleben this next few days and hopes that he is at home for Easter.

Here it is bitterly cold with six to eight degrees below freezing and one always has cold feet.

I have been to see Herr Grebe and he seems very ill. I do not think him likely to last long.

There is a deal of sickness here – diphtheria, typhus and smallpox. We have such a dearth of doctors as they are all at the front or in the lazaretts.

Rosie writes us that the smallpox is very bad in Celle, but here we have not much of that disease.

Wednesday 31st January.

We are having a terrible winter. Snow has been lying on the ground for nearly a fortnight and it snows a little more each day. When one cleans the front you find the next morning that there are a few inches more of snow. I wonder what the streets will be like when it thaws. We have had frost now for three weeks and the streets are in a fearful state.

One pities the poor horses for we have no men to clear the streets of snow and all is cleared from the pavement onto the road. The poor soldiers all seem to have frost in their feet and many are limping. What with the shortage of food, the shortage of clothes and coal, it is a very bad time we are all going through.

I have been very busy this past week paying calls and receiving visitors and then doing a little packing.

Arthur wrote me yesterday that he has hopes of going away soon for quite a number of prisoners leave Ruhleben in the next few days. I hope to leave here on the 6th and Arthur says he knows of one young lady who is to travel as far as London. I do hope I meet her for it seems not so certain about Mrs. Voight.

We are told that we cannot take any metal over the frontier for all is strictly forbidden.

Steinoff came to see me today and he was very sad at hearing that I was going away. He tells me that William is in Riga and it is twenty-five degrees below freezing. They constantly send him parcels and bread is what he asks for most.

Hermenia came to see me yesterday and she was upset at my going. All think that it will not be long before I come back again.

Herr Veury came last Sunday. He was in Ruhleben for one-and-a-half years and says that it will be six months before Arthur will be fit for any work. He himself was so afraid of the people and felt so very strange. He is only just feeling normal and it is nine months since he became free. He thinks this war must end soon. Many others say no and that it will last two more years. That is a dreadful outlook.

Saturday & Sunday 3rd & 4th February.

Up to now I have not received any notice of my papers and I think it is very improbable that I travel on the 6th.

I have a very great objection to travelling in March. Perhaps it will be April before I go.

I had a letter from the American Consul today, Sunday. He writes that it has complicated my leaving because I asked that if Arthur was not exchanged this month could my papers be made to travel on the 6th of any month. Perhaps it is all for the best that I do not travel. I am not in the best of condition and this dreadful weather is enough to frighten one off a journey. The trains are not heated as we are so short of coal.

I have never experienced such cold weather. Now it is over four weeks that we have been frozen up and it is impossible to get warm. This morning it was twenty degrees below freezing and for days the ice has never left the windows, not even in the rooms in which we live. We cannot look out on the streets and every shop and house is just as if they had been thickly whitened. It reminds me of the winter that James was born. Then we had the coal strike in England and all January and February there was skating and we had six weeks of frost. I remember it very well and we have never had such a winter since. Well, that cold was never as great as this. I even awake in the night shivering with cold. And in bed at that!

The poor soldiers fall down in the streets with the cold. I expect that they do not have enough warm food. One poor fellow fell by our door as he was marching past and some of his comrades fell over him. He was picked up quite unconscious.

There was a bread riot in and by Hamburg on Thursday and it has been very bad with the people. But what can a few women do?

I gave up my potatoes yesterday and they have only left me five pounds a week until the 15th of April. What we are to do from April until August no one knows.

The bread is now half barley meal and half swedes and it is awful stuff to eat. We hear that the swedes cannot last longer than April. The people say that February, March and April are to be our hunger months.

A great deal is written and talked of as regards the undersea boats and according to our papers England is now surrounded. I wonder if it is true and that England cannot do anything to help herself.

Arthur must have written about me being met at the frontier by the Women's Help Association for I have had a letter saying that I should be attended to. I am sorry if they have had their trouble for nothing. Mrs. Voight is like me, ready to travel at a few hours notice, but we still have no sign of the papers.

Monday 5th February.

I got a surprise today when I went to the police for they informed me that my papers were in Hannover and if I liked to go for them I could travel tomorrow. As there is so much unpleasantness over America I thought it better to risk it. But it meant being up half the night to get things in order. Belle and I ran over to Hannover and it took us from three o'clock till ten o'clock to get there and back.

It is now half past twelve at night and most of my luggage is on its way to the station thanks to Herr Roeder of the Weiner Hof. Luggage men are so difficult to obtain.

Tuesday 6th February.

I will leave here this morning at a quarter to seven and I hope for a successful journey.

I am just writing a letter to Arthur and pray that I shall soon meet him.

EPILOGUE

And that is how Annie's ancient diary ends...but the couple were reunited and did live happily ever after up to a point.

For during his time in Germany Arthur had been advised to invest his money in land, but at the end of the conflict and after five war loans his meadows were virtually worthless.

Arthur's health stood up well during his internment, but Annie was not so fortunate the stresses and strains of life in Germany during the Great War left her thin and unwell upon her return.

After 'borrowing' money from the family they again set up home in Stockport, Cheshire with a new address at 249 Stockport Road in Cheadle Heath – where they supplemented their income by taking in lodgers.

Their return to England was greeted by a relieved family and understandably Annie's welcome home was greater than that of Arthur's as the nation had lost many sons in the conflict.

As things began to return to normal a quantity of splendid furniture, paintings and treasures (some given by the Kaiser) eventually arrived in Stockport from Germany, but these possessions slowly disappeared as Arthur continued to indulge his passions for fine wine and bridge.

Arthur found gainful employment on the Manchester Ship Canal – where his command of languages landed him the post of translator.

Sadly, he did not take too well to his lesser position in life though he did admit it was far less stressful than his final three years in Germany.

Annie took everything in her stride. She began working in the church and maintained that she was far happier washing the tea-towels and looking after the poor of the parish than she ever was as the **grande chatelaine** in Germany.

Of their war years in Germany she was typically understated and always said: 'It was quite an adventure'.

Though sadly they did take their toll and although she saw the start of World War Two Annie only survived until 1940 when she passed away peacefully aged 66. Arthur – who envisaged an early end to the Second World War – survived a decade longer than his wife and finally surrendered in his sleep in 1950.

Until his dying day at the grand old age of 79 Arthur pined daily for the love of his life Annie. Now they are together forever – buried side by side in a Stockport cemetery.

Lightning Source UK Ltd.
Milton Keynes UK
UKOW040138110513

210526UK00001B/5/P